Ginat
egoz

THOUGHTS ON THE
PARASHAH

BY

Rabbi Eliyahu Attias

ISBN 1-892692-43-0

Printed by Sefer Press 732-606-2589

Printed in the United States of America

Contents

Introduction

WITH DEEP GRATITUDE TO Hashem, I present this collection of insights on the weekly Parashah.

A milestone in Torah study is celebrated with a festive dinner, as the Midrash[1] learns from Shelomo HaMelech:

> In Givon, Hashem appeared to Shelomo in a dream of the night. God said to him, "Request what I should give to you."
>
> Shelomo said, "Grant Your servant an understanding heart...."
>
> God said to him, "...Behold, I have given you a wise and understanding heart...."
>
> Shelomo.... came to Jerusalem..., sacrificed burnt offerings and peace offerings, and made a banquet for all his servants.[2]

I fondly recall Simhat Torah in the Lakewood Yeshiva. By the time we finished all the day's prayers and *hakafot,* the sun had already set. Our Rosh Yeshiva, Rav Aharon Kotler *ztz"l,* urged us to eat a festive meal — not in honor of Yom Tov, since it was already after sunset, but in honor of completing the yearly cycle of the public Torah reading.

What exactly are we rejoicing over when we complete a milestone in Torah study? And how do we learn to make a festive dinner from Shelomo? His banquet was made before he had completed anything!

I suggest one answer to both questions. Shelomo HaMelech

---

1. *Kohelet Rabbah* 1:1.
2. Melachim 1 3:5–15.

rejoiced at having received wisdom with which to understand Hashem's Torah, His mitzvot, and His creation. When we complete a Talmudic tractate, we rejoice at having acquired familiarity with its principles and laws, which will enable us to learn it better next time. And on Simhat Torah, we rejoice at having acquired the background for deepening our understanding of the weekly Parashah in the coming year.

Indeed, as we go through the weekly Parashah again each year, we can and should delve deeper and deeper into it.

The story is told of a man who brought his eight-year-old grandson to the rabbi and said proudly, "This child understands Humash and Rashi as well as I do."

"It's wonderful that the child understands Torah like the grandfather," said the rabbi. "But how unfortunate that the grandfather understands Torah like the child!"

HUMASH
Vayikra

PARASHAT
Vayikra

BEYOND THE SACRIFICES

When a man among you brings a sacrifice to Hashem....[1]

Here we begin Humash Vayikra and the laws of sacrifices. On account of our sins, we have no Temple in which to offer sacrifices now, but we do have a substitute — Torah study. The Gemara states: Whoever learns about the sacrifices is considered as if he has brought sacrifices, for it is written, "This is the Torah of the burnt-offering, the meal-offering, the sin-offering....[2]

The Navi goes even further; it teaches that we have something even greater than sacrifices:

"*Shemoʾa* is better than a choice sacrifice; to listen, than the fat of rams."[3]

Shemoʾa means "hear," "understand," and "obey."

These key words were spoken by the prophet Shemuel to Shaul, the first king of Israel.

Shemuel had delivered Hashem's command to Shaul: "Now go smite Amalek and obliterate everything it has. You shall not have

---

1. Vayikra 1:2.
2. Vayikra 7:37.
3. Shemuel 1 15:22.

pity on it. You shall put [all of it] to death, from man to woman, from infant to suckling, from ox to sheep, from camel to donkey.[4]

Shaul went to war and destroyed Amalek — except for its king, Agag, whom he planned to kill, and the best livestock, which he planned to sacrifice to Hashem, on the next day.

The next day, before Shaul had carried out these plans, Shemuel came, and the following exchange ensued.[5]

Shaul: "...I have fulfilled Hashem's word."

Shemuel: "And what is this sound of the sheep...? ...Why did you not obey...?"

Shaul: "But I did obey...."

Shaul claimed that he had fulfilled Hashem's command perfectly, for by that day's end, nothing and no one would remain of Amalek. Perhaps he even wanted to leave Shemuel a share in the mitzvah. Is one day's delay considered disobeying — especially when no time limit accompanied the command?

Yes! said Shemuel. True, you weren't given a time limit, but you should have understood that Hashem wanted no delay.

Had Shaul given up his own will, desires, and thoughts, in other words, sacrificed himself, to Hashem's Will, he would have understood that Hashem wanted no delay.

But Shaul, righteous though he was, filtered the command through his own outlook, as the Gemara[6] explains the verse "Shaul came to the city of Amalek, *vayarev banahal* — and he fought in the valley."[7] The Gemara expounds: Don't interpret "He fought in the valley" rather, "He quarreled about the valley," saying, "If when a single person is found slain, the Torah commands that a calf be

---

4. Shemuel 1 15:3.
5. Shemuel 1 15:13–21.
6. *Yoma* 22b.
7. Shemuel 1 15:5.

slaughtered in a valley as atonement,[8] surely we should not kill all these people! Furthermore, if the men sinned, did the animals sin?"

Shemuel reprimanded Shaul: The real reason you left the animals alive is because you pitied them, therefore you planned to offer them as sacrifices which is not "destruction." You also had pity on the king,[9] although you were explicitly commanded not to have pity on Amalek. Since you did not give up your own thoughts and feelings, you were unable to understand Hashem's Will.

Shemuel continued: Had you surrendered your entire mind and being to Hashem, you would have understood correctly. *Shemo'a* is better than bringing sacrifices.

The following anecdote illustrates that what a person hears is filtered through his world outlook.

Hafetz Hayyim *zt"l* sent regards to Rabbi Meir Simhah *zt"l*, author of the *Ohr Sameah*, with a Jew who was traveling from Radin to Dvinsk.

The traveler arrived in Dvinsk, went to Rabbi Meir Simhah, and brought the regards.

"Please tell the Hafetz Hayyim," said Rabbi Meir Simhah, "that he should walk barefoot carrying stones on his shoulders."

The traveler was appalled. Upon returning to Radin, he tried to avoid the Hafetz Hayyim so that he would not have to deliver the message. Eventually, though, the Hafetz Hayyim encountered him in the street and asked, "Did you go to Rabbi Meir Simhah? What did he say?"

The traveler reluctantly repeated what he had been told.

"Amen!" said the Hafetz Hayyim fervently. "He wished me that I merit to see Mashiah and serve as Kohen Gadol, wearing

---

8. Reference is to the eglah arufah; see Devarim 21:9.
9. As Ahav king of Israel would later have pity on his enemy Ben Hadad king of Aram; see Melachim 1 20:33.

the stones of the breastplate and walking barefoot in the restored Temple."

We can imagine that the traveler, surprised and relieved, asked himself, "Why didn't I understand it that way?"

However, because the Hafetz Hayyim was connected to the final redemption, always having it on his mind and even authoring a work about the laws of sacrifices,[10] he understood.

Similarly, Hashem sends all of us messages and if we are connected to Him we will understand. Our Sages said: If afflictions strike a person, he should examine his deeds. The commentators explain that he should examine them in light of the measure-for-measure principle. Since Hashem sends the punishment that corresponds precisely to the sin, the afflicted person can know what his sin was.

But there is a catch: To understand the message that Hashem is sending him through the afflictions, he must be connected to Hashem, and his filter must be clean. He must believe that whatever Hashem does is for the best, and that everything that happens is done by Him.

It is told that the wise men of Helm were amazed to hear about a new invention: a wagon that did not need to be drawn by horses. "How is such a thing possible?" they asked one another. "If there are no horses, what pulls it?"

After grave deliberation, they decided to send the wisest among them to investigate the new invention. He went to the big city, where he carefully observed the train. Then he returned to Helm and reported his findings.

"I managed to understand 98%," he told his eager listeners. "Only 2% remains a mystery.

---

10. *Yalkut Halachot* on *Kodshim*.

"This is how it works. The last car moves because it is pulled by the car in front of it, and the next to last moves because it is pulled by the one in front of *it*, and so on. The only thing I don't understand is... what pulls the first car."

In a way, we are like the wise men of Helm. We don't understand that everything that happens is "pulled" by Hashem alone. He is the primary Cause, the Reason behind all reasons, Who pulls the strings behind all events, situations, and conditions in His world.

Once we internalize this, we can nullify our own thoughts and desires before Him. Then we will be able to hear His message, understand, and obey. And "*shemoa* is better than a choice sacrifice" — offering up our selves entirely to Hashem is greater than offering up an animal sacrifice.

A PLEASING AROMA

A fire-offering, a pleasing aroma to Hashem.[11]

What is meant by "a pleasing aroma to Hashem"?

In these mysterious words, says the Ramban, lies the *ta'am*[12] of the sacrifices.

The Ramban also cites the reason for the sacrifices offered by the Rambam in *Moreh Nevuchim*, and refutes his view.

The Rambam says that Egyptians and the Babylonians, in whose lands the Jews lived, worshiped livestock. The Egyptians worshiped the lamb, while the Babylonians worshiped demons, which appeared to them in the guise of he-goats. And to this day cows are

---

11. Vayikra 1:9.
12. Literally, "taste." The true reason for any mitzvah is that Hashem so commanded.

not slaughtered in India. Hashem commanded us to sacrifice these three species to Him in order to cure wrong beliefs and atone for sins.

The Ramban objects on two counts: To say that the sacrifices come only to remove wrong beliefs from the hearts of the wicked and foolish is an insult to Hashem's Altar! Besides, before idolatry came on the scene, Adam's son Hevel sacrificed the best of his flock, "and Hashem turned to Hevel and to his offering."[13] And even before Egyptians or Babylonians came on the scene, when Noah left the Ark after the Flood he offered a sacrifice; and "Hashem smelled the pleasing aroma," on account of which "Hashem said in His heart, 'I will not again... smite every living....'"[14]

We can explain the reasoning of the Rambam as follows.

Indeed, the concept of a sacrifice existed from the beginning of human history. Hashem was pleased with the sacrifices of Hevel and Noah because they conveyed their readiness to give up everything for the Creator, even their very life, because the animal sacrificed is a symbolic substitute for this. This is what the Torah calls "a pleasing aroma to Hashem."

Rambam[15] teaches us that the generation of Adam's grandson Enosh made a grave error, saying, "Since Hashem created stars and planets to rule the world, setting them in the heavens and sharing His glory with them, it must be His Will that we honor them. For by honoring the King's servants, one honors the King."

As time went on, they sank lower and said, "Hashem commanded men to worship the stars."

Apparently, from there they sank even lower until they worshiped sheep, cows, and demons.

---

13. Bereshit 4:4.
14. Bereshit 8:21.
15. *Hilchot Avodah Zarah.*

What was wrong, with the original thought? Didn't they serve the heavenly bodies for Hashem's honor?

In truth, this thought was rooted in wickedness, they did not want to approach Hashem directly because they did not want to humble themselves before Him and be subservient to Him.

Picture a subject who is granted an audience with his king, who has the power of life and death in his hands and rules over a great kingdom. As the subject enters the throne room, he trembles in fear and awe. Every vestige of pride and self-interest vanish. He stands ready and waiting to do the king's bidding. He has nullified himself before the king.

But when the same subject stands before the king's clerk, he does not give up his pride and self-interest; he does not tremble. He even jokes with the clerk.

Thus the generation of Enosh were not honoring the heavenly bodies in order to honor Hashem, as they claimed, but in order to avoid nullifying themselves before Him.

Offering sacrifices was a way of restoring the original situation, where the person is ready to sacrifice everything for Hashem and dispel the foolish thoughts of the Egyptians and Babylonians in whose lands the Jews lived.

A perfect example is the Pesach offering in Egypt. The Jews were commanded to take a lamb, the Egyptian diety; to barbecue it, sending its unmistakable aroma wafting through Egypt; and to keep the bones intact, so that the Egyptians would recognize their deity's limbs. Thus the Pesach offering helped the Jews detach themselves from the Egyptian way of thinking, return to the Creator, and totally nullify themselves before Him.

Now we can understand the Rambam's teaching that the *ta'am* of the sacrifices was to cure the wrong beliefs that had been adopted by mankind, beginning with the decision of Enosh's generation that Hashem should not be approached directly, and continuing downhill until the lamb was worshiped in ancient Egypt and the cow is worshiped today in India. By bringing sacrifices to Hashem, men go back to nullifying themselves before Him as they did in the days of Adam and Hevel. This is the "pleasing aroma to Hashem."

Zachor and Parah

REMEMBER!

Zachor: Remember what Amalek did to you, on the way, when you left Egypt....[1]

Parah: This is the decree of the Torah.... They shall take to you a completely red cow....[2]

Reading Parashat Zachor is obviously a mitzvah of the Torah; we are commanded, "Remember what Amalek did to you...." But what about reading Parashat Parah?

Tosafot, cited by *Bet Yosef*, states that this, too, is a mitzvah of the Torah. But the Vilna Gaon says that this must be a copier's error — since there is no commandment in the Torah to remember the red cow!

However, there is a command to remember the sin of the golden calf,[3] as it says, "Remember, do not forget, that you angered Hashem, your God, in the desert...."[4] *Yalkut Yosef* explains that this command is connected to Parah: Thus the Torah commands us to remember

---

1. Devarim 25:17.
2. Bamidbar 19 2.
3. See Devarim 9:8–21.
4. Devarim 9:7

the sin of the golden calf, but since it is a disgrace for the Jewish people, we read Parashat Parah instead. For rhe red cow comes to atone for the sin of the golden calf, as Rashi[5] says: The matter may be likened to a maidservant's son who soiled the king's palace. They say, "Let his mother come and clean the excrement." Similarly, let the cow come and atone for the calf.

From here, we may extrapolate to Parashat Zachor. Just as a veiled rebuke lies behind the reading of Parah, so is there a rebuke behind the reading of Zachor.

The Midrash[6] relates a parable: A king kept a watchdog in his vineyard to bite anyone who dared break the fence. One day, the kings' son broke the fence and was bitten. Thereafter, whenever the king wished to remind his son of his misdeed, he would say, "Remember how the dog bit you."

Similarly, the Torah relates that when the Jewish people were in Rephidim, they sinned, "saying, 'Is Hashem among us or not?' and Amalek came and fought Israel in Rephidim."[7] Thereafter, whenever Hashem wished to remind the Jewish people of their sin in Rephidim, He would say, "Remember what Amalek did to you."

From here we see that the purpose of reading Zachor is to remember our own lack of faith, much as the purpose of reading Parah is to remember our sin with the golden calf.

Our Sages mention another sin committed in Rephidim. This sin is hinted in the word *Rephidim* — an acronym of *raphu yedehem,* "their hands were slack" in Torah study.

What does slacking in Torah study mean? This we learn from the Rambam's[8] teaching that the Torah does not endure in someone

---

5. Bamidbar 19:22, citing Rabbi Moshe HaDarshan.
6. *Tanhuma,* Ki Tzetei 9.
7. Shemot 17:7–8.
8. *Hilchot Talmud Torah* 3:12.

who indulges in food, sleep, vacations, and other physical pleasures, but only in someone who kills himself over Torah study.

Slacking in Torah study is dangerous, says the Gemara.[9] "If you slacked, in a day of affliction your strength will be limited"[10] — for the angels will not strengthen you.[11]

Reading about Amalek's attack, which came in response to our two sins in Rephidim, is a powerful reminder to shore up our faith in Hashem as well as our toil in His Torah.

---

9. *Berachot* 63a.
10. Mishlei 24:10.
11. Rashi, Mishlei 24:10.

Shabbat HaGadol

PROUD TO BE A JEW

From the Haftarah:

> Your words have become harsh against Me, says Hashem.
> You say, "What have we spoken against You?"
> You have said, "It is useless to serve God. What gain is there in our having kept His watch and walking submissively before Hashem...?"[1]

The *Shulhan Aruch* makes a puzzling statement:[2]

> The Shabbat before Pesach is called Shabbat HaGadol ("the great Shabbat") because of the miracle that took place on it.

Why is this point recorded in our code of Jewish law? And why does a miracle justify calling this Shabbat "great"?

The *Mishnah Berurah* describes the miracle: When the Jews were about to leave Egypt, Hashem commanded them, "On the tenth of [Nissan], they shall take for themselves... a lamb...."[3] The Egyptians saw and asked, "What are you doing?" They replied, "We are going to slaughter it for the Pesach offering, as Hashem commanded us." The Egyptians were furious about the Jews slaughtering their deities

---

1. Malachi 3:13–14.
2. *Siman* 430.
3. Shmot 12:3.

but were powerless to take action. And that year, the tenth of Nissan fell on Shabbat.

Now let's go a step further.

The Rambam[4] writes that a human being is naturally drawn after the outlook and deeds of the people in his environment. Accordingly, the Jewish people, who had been living in Egypt for 210 years, had surely been influenced by the outlook of the Egyptians — who looked up to the lamb and down at the Jew. Hashem commanded them to take the lambs four days early so that each one would be proud to be a Jew and to fulfill Hashem's commands.

When a boy turns bar mitzvah, he becomes obligated in all the mitzvot — yet a special emphasis is placed on the mitzvah of tefillin. Why? Because the head-tefillin are a crown, which we to refer in the blessing *oter Yisrael betifarah*, "Who crowns Israel with splendor."

A Jew wears the crown of tefillin because he is a king, as Hashem said before giving us the Torah: "You shall be to me a kingdom of priests...."[5] It is crucial that the bar mitzvah boy be proud of keeping the Torah and mitzvot that Hashem gave us.

When the British ruled Palestine, they sentenced two Jews to be hanged for trying to oust them. The renowned tzaddik Rabbi Aryeh Levin *zt"l* visited Barzani and Finkelstein in jail. He brought them tefillin and explained the importance of this crown and how proud we Jews are to be kings. Encouraged by the thought of being executed as proud Jews, they kissed the tefillin again and again.

The Gemara[6] says that there are three who are bold: Israel among the nations, the dog among animals, and the rooster among fowl. What is their boldness? Says Rashi: That they cannot be vanquished.

That is, all three have a mission from which they cannot be

---

4. Hilchot De'ot 6:1.
5. Shemot 19:6.
6. *Betzah* 25b.

budged. We say in our morning blessing, "Who gave the rooster understanding to distinguish between day and night." The rooster was given the mission of calling out to wake men up in the morning, and it cannot be stopped. The dog is loyal to its master and cannot be budged from this loyalty. Similarly, the Jewish people remain loyal to Hashem.

In the Haftarah of Shabbat HaGadol, the prophet rebukes the Jewish people in Hashem's Name for speaking harshly against Him, saying, "It is useless to serve God. What gain is there in our having kept His watch and walking submissively before Hashem...?"

But if the Jews spoke such harsh words, how could they ask, "What have we spoken against You?"

The Mussar authorities explain as follows. Suppose two young men are asked, "What do you do?" One answers proudly, "I study in university." If the other answers weakly, "I learn in yeshiva," it is as if he had said, "It is useless to serve God."

How tragic this is! The Gemara[7] says: "In hidden chambers, My soul weeps because of pride"[8] — because of the loss of Jewish pride.

The yeshiva student should declare with pride, "In my merit, the Jewish nation endures! In my merit, the whole world exists!"

The main miracle of Shabbat HaGadol is that when the Jews dragged the Egyptian deities through the streets of Egypt they stopped feeling inferior to the Egyptians and started taking pride again in being the offspring of Avraham, Yitzhak and Yaakov.

Shabbat HaGadol, which might be translated "the Shabbat of greatness," calls on us to recognize our personal greatness, remember that we are kings, and take pride in being Jewish.

---

7. *Hagigah* 5b.
8. Yirmiyahu 13:17.

PARASHAT

Tzav

THE PLACE OF THE SIN-OFFERING

In the place where the burnt-offering is slaughtered shall the sin-offering be slaughtered....[1]

Why are the animals for sin-offerings and for burnt-offerings slaughtered in the same place in the Temple Courtyard?

Mussaf Rashi answers: So that people seeing the animal slaughtered will not know if it is a sin-offering, and the sinner will not be shamed.

We might add that one should avoid looking at a sinner, for seeing him will have a powerful negative impact. Thus our Sages said that whoever sees a *sotah*[2] in her disgrace should [elevate himself by] separating himself from wine. We find no such obligation when one only hears of a *sotah*. This is because seeing can have a negative influence on him and requires additional protection from sin.

The Midrash[3] relates that the father of a certain pious man was an alcoholic. One day as the pious man was walking to the synagogue, he saw a drunkard in disgrace. He went and brought

---

1. Vayikra 7:2.
2. Wayward woman.
3. Tanhuma, Shemini 11.

his father to see, in the hope that he would learn a lesson. Instead, the father went over to the drunkard and asked him, "Where did you buy your drinks?"

Seeing something toward which we are already inclined strengthens our inclination, even if we see the disgrace in it.

This explains why the Torah says, "You are standing today... before Hashem... for you to pass into the covenant of Hashem... For you know how we dwelled in... Egypt... and you saw their abominations and their disgusting idols...."[4] Even though the idols were not only false but also extremely repugnant, a covenant was necessary to keep the Jews from idolatry because of the power of seeing.

On the last night that the Jewish people were in Egypt, when the Egyptian firstborn were smitten, the Jews were commanded, "No man shall leave the entrance of his house until morning."[5] Rashi explains: Because the angel of destruction would not distinguish between a Jew and an Egyptian.

But, as we say in the Haggadah, "The Jews were *metzuyanim* there" — they stood out strikingly in Egypt. If so, how could the angel fail to recognize them?

Because any Jew who wanted to go out for a last sightseeing stroll in Egypt before leaving was connected to Egypt, and deliberately looking at Egypt would tie him to it even more. An angel, who sees only a person's inner self and not his exterior, would see him as an Egyptian, for a person is defined by his will.

The negative and positive effects of seeing are illustrated by the placement of signs at the crossroads. Signs pointing toward the cities of refuge were hung at every crossroads for the benefit of unintentional

---

4. Parashat Nitzavim, Devarim 29:9–16.
5. Shemot 12:22.

murderers fleeing there; but no signs pointing to Jerusalem were hung for the benefit of pilgrims. Why? So that the pilgrims would ask directions, but the murderers would not. It is harmful to see a killer; but there is great benefit in seeing Jews fulfilling the mitzvah of going up to Jerusalem for the festivals.

Of the mitzvah of tzitzit, the Torah says, "And you shall see it and remember all of Hashem's mitzvot."[6] Our Sages explain that seeing the *techelet*-colored thread on it reminds a person of the heavens, where the Heavenly Throne is, and hence of all Hashem's mitzvot.

How wondrous it is that we can use our sense of sight to cleave to Hashem!

We conclude with a comment of the Baal Shem Tov: If one sees another committing a sin, very likely Hashem is showing him that he is falling short in that area.

---

6. Bamidbar 15:39.

PARASHAT

Shemini

JOY AND SORROW

It was on the eighth day.... Aaron's sons Nadav and Avihu... brought before Hashem an alien fire that He had not commanded them... and they died before Hashem. Moshe said to Aaron, "Of this did Hashem speak, saying, 'I will be sanctified through those closest to Me....'"[1]

How the people rejoiced at the inauguration of the Mishkan![2] But on the eighth day, when the joy climaxed, tragedy struck: Aaron's two saintly sons went into the Holy of Holies to offer incense and were consumed by a heavenly fire.

The Midrash[3] focuses on the bereaved mother. The joy of Elisheva, says the Midrash, had surpassed that of all women of her time. For she was the sister of Nahshon ben Aminidav, head of the Tribe of Yehudah; the sister-in-law of Moshe Rabbenu; the wife of Aaron, the Kohen Gadol; and the mother of four Kohanim. Suddenly, two of her sons died.

---

1. Vayikra 9:1,10:1–3.
2. Tabernacle.
3. *Tanhuma, ot 2.*

Of this it is written, "Do not rejoice excessively."[4] For joy does not remain with a person. Not everyone who rejoices today will rejoice tomorrow; [on the other hand,] not everyone who grieves today will grieve tomorrow....

The Midrash teaches that Hashem made man's condition in this world unstable. Occasions for joy give way to occasions for grief, and vice versa. Man's circumstances here are as temporary as his life is.

Why?

Rashi[5] on Parashat Vayeshev comments: Yaakov Avinu sought to dwell in tranquility, and the tragedy of Yoseph struck him. Said Hashem, "Isn't what awaits the righteous in the world to come enough for them, that they seek to dwell in tranquility in this world?"

Accordingly, tragedies remind us that our true home is in the world that is entirely good, and we are here only to prepare for it.

In a similar vein, Shelomo HaMelech said, "In every sorrow, there will be gain."[6] How so?

Sorrow protects a person from excessive joy, which might have drawn him after worldly pleasure and away from the Creator,[7] and make him appear to be casting off the Yoke of the Kingdom of Heaven.[8] So Hashem sometimes brings a sobering experience on a person for his own good, to keep him under the Yoke.

Although Shelomo HaMelech also "praised joy"[9] — referring

4. Tehilim 75:5.
5. Bereshit 37:2.
6. Mishlei 14:24.
7. Rabbenu Yonah's disciples.
8. Rashi.
9. Kohelet 8:15.

to the joy of a mitzvah,[10] such as a wedding,[11] the Gemara relates that when Rav Ashi saw the Sages rejoicing greatly at his son's wedding, he broke a rare vessel in order to sadden them. Thus even the mitzvah of gladdening bride and groom should be kept within reasonable limits.

What, then, is the right course for us to take? The Gemara[12] answers: "Serve Hashem with fear, and rejoice with trembling."[13] In this world, it is forbidden to fill our mouth with laughter. But after the Final Redemption, it will be different: "When Hashem returns the captivity of Tzion... Then will our mouth be filled with laughter and our tongue with glad song."[14]

---

10. *Shabbat* 30b.
11. Rashi.
12. *Berachot* 31a.
13. Tehilim 2:11.
14. Tehilim 126:2.

PARASHAT

Tazria

THE COVENANT OF CIRCUMCISION

When a woman conceives and gives birth to a male....[1]

Rashi cites *Midrash Rabbah:*[2]

Just as the creation of man took place after that of animals, so are his laws stated after those of animals. The Torah says, "This is the law of the animal and the bird...."[3] and then "When a woman conceives and gives birth to a male...."

Why, though, was man created after the animals?
Answers *Midrash Tanhuma*:

So that if he is meritorious, he is told, "You were created last so that you would find everything ready for you."

And if he is not meritorious, he is told, "Even the mosquito preceded you [and is thus more important than you]."

Here we have two opposing lines of thought. How can man be told "Even the mosquito preceded you" when he really did find

---

1. Vayikra 12:1.
2. Citing *Vayikra Rabbah* 12:1.
3. Vayikra 11:46.

everything ready for him? And what does all this have to do with the mitzvah of circumcising a newborn boy?

We begin our search for the answer with a Gemara.[4] Rabbi Yehudah HaNassi said: An *am haaretz* is forbidden to eat meat, for it is written, *Zot Torat habehemah veha'of,* "This is the Torah of the animal and the bird...." Whoever learns Torah is allowed to eat meat; whoever does not is forbidden to eat it.

Why?

The reward for mitzvot is reserved for the world to come, which is eternal. But sometimes, writes Rabbi Yitzchak Belaser[5] in *Cochvei Ohr,* a person receives part of his reward in this world. He pays dearly for the good he has here; it's deducted from his merits and from his eternal good there.

This thought worried our greatest tzaddikim, starting with Yaakov Avinu, who said, "*Katonti mikol hahasadim*[6]— my merits have become diminished through the kindnesses that You have done for me."[7]

It worried Rabbi Akiva, too. The Gemara[8] relates that when Rabbi Eliezer became ill, his disciples came to visit him. They began to weep, but Rabbi Akiva laughed. When they asked him why, he replied, "As long as I saw that my teacher's wine, flax, oil, and honey never became ruined, I worried that perhaps he had received all his reward in this world. Now that I see him lying in pain, I am relieved."

It stands to reason that our merits will not be reduced if we take from this world only what we need to exist. Hashem provides for all living beings that He created, worthy or not.

---

4. *Pesahim* 49b.
5. *Ohr Yisrael, Cochvei Ohr,* Ch. 2.
6. Bereshit 32:11.
7. Rashi.
8. *Sanhedrin* 101a.

That is, He provides the necessities of life. For a human being, eating meat is not a necessity but a luxury. He can live on earth-grown produce and on dairy products. Eating these does not diminish his merits, and hence his reward — but eating meat is liable to do just that.

All this applies to an *am haaretz*. A Jew who toils in Torah is different. Eating meat does not reduce his merits because for him it is a necessity. It gives him the strength he needs to learn and teach Torah, as in the case of Rav Nahman. The Gemara[9] relates that one evening, Rava asked Rav Nahman a question in Halachah, which he could not answer. The following morning, he not only answered, but also explained why he had not been able to do so the previous evening. The reason was that he had not eaten meat that day (for he had been fasting[10]).

So eating meat is a necessity for Torah scholars. But for those who do not learn Torah, eating meat is a luxury, which is deducted from their reward in the world to come.

Now we can understand the Tanhuma. If a person learns Torah, he is told, "All the kosher animals are ready for you to eat, and you have a right to eat them." But if he does not learn Torah, he is told, "What right have you to slaughter an animal and eat it? That is a luxury, for which you will have to pay from your heavenly bank account."

If so, how can a person who is not in yeshiva eat meat?

A solution may be deduced from the Torah's account of the great famine. The Egyptians paid with their money and animals for the grain that Yosef had amassed for Pharaoh. When these resources were used up, they sold themselves, with their land, as serfs to Pharaoh.

---

9. *Bava Kamma* 71b.
10. *Tosafot.*

The priests were an exception. "Only the land of the priests he did not buy, for the priests had a stipend from Pharaoh...."[11]

If Pharaoh provided for the priests, surely Hashem provides for His servants! How does a Jew become Hashem's servant? By supporting Torah study to the best of his ability and sending his children to Torah schools. Then he can eat meat without having to pay from his heavenly bank account, for the King of kings feeds His servants meat.

When a person works for a company, the company pays his expenses. Thus we say on *Rosh HaShannah*, "Remember us for life...for Your sake...." — we live only for You; we work for Your company.

This explains why the Torah conveys the mitzvah of circumcision immediately after telling us what animals we may eat. At his *brit,* the new human being enters a covenant with Hashem; he becomes His servant who works for His company, and we pray that he will continue on this path always.

ALL ALONE

The person with *tzaraat*[12]... shall dwell in isolation, outside the camp....[13]

Our Sages teach that *tzaraat* would strike a person who spoke *lashon hara.*[14] We know that Hashem punishes measure for measure, to enable a person to figure out why he is suffering. How is *tzaraat* a measure-for-measure punishment for *lashon hara*?

---

11. Bereshit 47:22.
12. Although commonly translated "leprosy," *tzaraat* was a miraculous affliction that reflected a person's spiritual deficiency.
13. Vayikra 13:45–46.
14. Speaking against another even if what is said is true.

In order to answer, let's examine the famous passage from Tehilim[15] about guarding one's tongue:

> Who is the man who desires life...? Guard your tongue from evil...

This passage is puzzling. "Life" refers to the eternal life of the world to come, as it is written, "...My laws..., which a man shall carry out, and he shall live through them"[16] — in the world to come, as Rashi explains. The passage from Tehilim is saying: If you want Gan Eden, don't sin with *lashon hara*.

But that's not how the system works! To get into Gan Eden, you have to arrive with a suitcase full of mitzvot. Someone whose suitcase is full of sins is shown to Gehinnom. What the passage should have said is: "Who desires Gan Eden? Stockpile mitzvot. Who wants to avoid Gehinnom? Guard your tongue from evil." Why does it put Gan Eden together with guarding your tongue?

We may explain in light of an anecdote from the Hovot Ha-Levavot.[17]

Reuven, who had just spoken *lashon hara* against Shimon, was surprised to receive a gift from his victim. "What is this all about?" he asked Shimon.

"Today you sent me a gift, so I am sending you one in return," Shimon replied.

Unwittingly, Reuven had sent Shimon a very great gift — all his mitzvot! For when someone speaks *lashon hara*, the credit for all his mitzvot is transferred to the victim. As if that weren't enough, the victim's debt of sins is transferred to the perpetrator.

---

15. Tehilim 34:13–14.
16. Vayikra 18:5.
17. *Shaar HaKeniah*, ch. 7.

Thus David prayed, "Let me not be disgraced by a scoundrel"[18] — If I must be disgraced through *lashon hara,* let it not be by a scoundrel who has no mitzvot for me to take![19]

This explains why "the man who desires life" is told, "Guard your tongue from evil." If you want Gan Eden, make sure you don't lose your mitzvot by speaking against others.

Now let's return to our original question: How is *tzaraat* a measure-for-measure punishment for *lashon hara*?

The *metzora*[20] is cut off from family and friends. He dwells alone outside the camp, separated even from the company of other *metzora'im*. His only visitors are wolves, rats, and the like.

This scene is a semblance of his world to come. He will dwell there alone. Who will visit him? Not the good angels created from his mitzvot, for they were transferred to his victim. Only the bad angels that were created from his sins and from the sins of his victim.

Contemplating this should prompt the *metzora* to regret his sin and repent — and prompt us to stay far away from *lashon hara*. As we go through life filling our suitcase with mitzvot to take to Gan Eden, let's make sure we don't lose it on the way. "Who is the man who desires life? Guard your tongue from evil!"

---

18. Tehilim 39:9.
19. Hida.
20. Person afflicted with *tzaraat*.

Metzora

WHO GOES TO WHOM?

This shall be *torat hametzora,* the law of the *metzora,* on the day of his purification. He shall be brought to the Kohen.[1]

This verse says that the *metzora* goes to the Kohen, but the next verse says that the Kohen goes to the *metzora.*

The Kohen shall go outside the camp; the Kohen shall look, and behold, the *tzaraat* affliction had been healed from the *metzora.*

Who goes to whom? And how can we understand the contradiction between the two verses?

I would answer that the second verse gives practical instructions. Since the *metzora* must stay outside the camp until the Kohen purifies him, the Kohen must go out to him. The first verse presents *torat hametzora,* which may be understood: "the teaching of the *metzora.*" This teaching may be learned from the Rambam.[2]

Tzaraat... is not a natural matter, but a sign and a wonder among the Jewish people in order to warn them against *lashon hara.*
For he who speaks *lashon hara,* the walls of his house undergo

---

1. Vayikra 14:2.
2. *Hilchot Tumat Tzaraat* 16:10.

changes. If he repents, the house is purified. If he remains in his wickedness, the... vessels of his home... undergo changes.... If he remains in his wickedness..., his garments undergo changes.... If he remains in his wickedness... he becomes a *metzora*. Then he is separated, publicized [that is, as he leaves the camp, he must proclaim, "Impure! Impure"] and isolated until he no longer engages in the conversation of the wicked, which is scoffing and *lashon hara*.

Regarding this, the Torah warns, "Beware of a *tzaraat* affliction.... Remember what Hashem... did to Miriam."[3] The verse is saying: Contemplate what befell the prophetess Miriam, who spoke about her brother [Moshe]. She... had risked her life to save him from the sea; and she did not speak ill of him, but rather erred in comparing him to other prophets.... Even so, she was immediately afflicted with *tzaraat*.

All the more so foolish evildoers, who speak excessively.... Therefore it is proper for a person... to distance himself from sitting with them and speaking with them so that he will not be trapped in... their foolishness. And this is the way of the sitting of the wicked scoffers: At first they talk a lot of nonsense.... From this, they come to speak ill of the righteous....

But the conversation of righteous Jewish people is only in matters of Torah and wisdom. Therefore Hashem helps them..., as it is written, "Then those who fear Hashem spoke to one another, and Hashem listened and heard, and a book of remembrance was written before him...."[4]

So the speaker of *lashon hara* is sent out of the camp to disconnect him from the company of wicked scoffers. Accordingly, we may explain the first verse: "This shall be the teaching of the *metzora*.... He shall be brought to the Kohen[5] — he shall abandon

---

3. Devarim 24:8–9.
4. Malachi 3:9.
5. Vayikra 14:2.

his old circle of friends and join only those who fear Hashem, such as the Kohen, who is a righteous Torah scholar.

But I have a question on the Rambam. Our Sages say that *tzaraat* is inflicted on a person for speaking *lashon hara*, but the Rambam says "scoffing and *lashon hara*." On what basis does he add "scoffing"?

Perhaps it is because if not for the scoffing, the *lashon hara* could have been corrected through rebuke and *tzaraat* would not have been necessary.

The *Mesilat Yesharim*[6] analyzes the problem with scoffing: Jesting and scoffing deflect rebuke from entering a person's heart, much as oil smeared on a shield deflects arrows. Even one instance of scoffing can deflect many rebukes. No wonder our Sages said that scoffers bring suffering upon themselves, as it is written, "Judgments are prepared for the scoffers, and blows for the backs of fools."[7] This is only logical; since scoffers laugh off rebukes, they must be corrected by pain, which cannot be laughed off.

So the scoffer who spoke *lashon hara* is afflicted with *tzaraat* and sent outside the camp to live in isolation. This gives him the opportunity to contemplate his wrongdoing and repent.

The Midrash[8] comments that *tzaraat* and similar impurities are inflicted on a person in his youth to prompt him to contemplate, as it is written, "And remember your Creator in the days of your youth."[9] But old age provides its own type of contemplation. Hashem says to man, "I am pure, My abode is pure, My servants are pure, and the soul that I gave you is pure. Make sure to return it to Me as pure as I gave it to you."[10]

---

6. Ch. 5.
7. Mishlei 19:29.
8. *Vayikra Rabbah* 18:1.
9. Kohelet 12:1.
10. See also Rabbenu Yonah, *Shaarei Teshuvah, shaar* 2, *ot* 7.

THE CHIRPING OF BIRDS

The Kohen shall command, and two live, clean birds... shall be taken for the person being purified.[11]

Says Rashi: Since *tzaraat* strikes on account of *lashon hara*, which is a deed of chatter, purification requires birds, which chirp continuously.

How are men speaking *lashon hara* comparable to birds chirping?

It seems that both birds and men have an urge to use their voice, and that they take pleasure in using it.

Men find silence uncomfortable, so they chatter without restriction, like birds. And to make the conversation interesting, they include *lashon hara*.

In other words, *lashon hara* is rooted in the natural human desire to speak, which is similar to the desire to eat or sleep.

This concept is supported by the Daat Zekenim's comment on the verse "Miriam and Aharon spoke about Moshe":[12] "Since women are talkers, and Miriam spoke more than Aharon, the verse puts her first and she was stricken more."

The Gemara[13] tells us how to handle our desire to speak:

What is man's craft in this world? He should make himself as one who is mute [that is, he must train himself to be mute].

Why doesn't the Gemara say simply, "He should be silent"?

Because the point is not to be silent, but to be mute when it comes to *lashon hara*.

A person can be guilty of *lashon hara* without speaking a word. A gesture of the hand, a movement of the head, or a wink of the

---

11. Vayikra 14:4.
12. Bamidbar 12:1.
13. *Hulin* 89a.

eyes can also convey deprecation. So can the wrinkling of a nose, as hinted in the verse *ki be'apam hargu ish*,[14] "With their nose, they killed a man."[15]

On the other hand, it is possible to speak much and still be mute in the area of *lashon hara*.

It is told that the Hafetz Hayyim once heard a few travelers speaking against the *gabbai* of a synagogue. He went over to them and started a long conversation about horses. Later, when asked why he had wasted so much time speaking about horses, the Hafetz Hayyim replied, "It is better for Jews to speak about horses than about other people."

The Hafetz Hayyim had channeled these travelers' urge to speak into neutral, harmless areas. Had it been possible, he would surely have channeled it into positive, productive ones. These are discussed by the Gemara after it tells us to be mute:

> Does this apply also to words of Torah?
> We are taught: "You shall speak *tzedek*."[16]

Tzedek, "righteousness," refers to the Torah,[17] which is the ultimate *tzedek*. *Tzedek* is also the root of *tzedakah*, "charity." It is a mitzvah to use our urge to speak in studying Torah aloud — and if we explain Torah to someone in need of an explanation, we acquire the mitzvah of charity as well.

We can also give rein to our urge to speak by comforting the poor and encouraging and downcast. A person who does this mitzvah, says the Gemara,[18] brings upon himself eleven blessings!

---

14. Bereshit 49:6.
15. Hafetz Hayyim.
16. Tehilim 58:2.
17. Rashi on the Gemara.
18. *Bava Batra* 9b.

PARASHAT

Aharei Mot

INTENTIONS

You shall safeguard My decrees and My laws, which a person shall carry out, *vahai bahem*, and through them he will live. *Ani Hashem,* I am Hashem.[1]

What should our intention be when fulfilling mitzvot?

We find conflicting answers. In fact, the Rambam and the *Mesilat Yesharim* seem to contradict themselves on this point!

FOR THE REWARD

One answer comes from our verse, as explained by Rashi: *Vahai bahem* — through them he will live in the world to come. *Ani Hashem* — I, Hashem, am reliable about paying reward.

Further proof that we are to choose good and fulfill mitzvot with the intention of meriting Gan Eden comes from the verse, "Life and death have I set before you... and you shall choose life."[2] Rashi comments: This is like a man telling his son, "Choose yourself a good portion in my estate...."

---

1. Vayikra 18:4–5.
2. Devarim 30:19.

Similarly, the Rambam³ says that Jews long for the Messianic era because once they are free of oppression, they will be able to study Torah and fulfill mitzvot unhindered in order to merit Gan Eden.

And the *Mesilat Yesharim* begins by saying: The foundation of piety and the root of perfect service is for a person to know clearly what his obligation is in this world, and toward what goal he must aim in all that he does throughout his life. Our Sages taught that a person is created only to delight in Hashem and enjoy the radiance of His Shechinah, and the means by which a person reaches this goal is the mitzvot.

But there is an opposing view.

NOT FOR THE REWARD

Our Sages⁴ said:

> Be not like servants who serve their master in order to receive a reward. Instead, be like servants who serve their master not in order to receive a reward....

The Rambam⁵ quotes this Mishnah and tells us: Do not learn Torah and fulfill mitzvot in order to become rich, to be called 'Rabbi," or to receive reward in the world to come. And do not keep away from sins in order to be spared the curses that are written in the Torah or in order not to be cut off from eternal life. This is serving Hashem out of fear, which is not the level of the wise. Rather, we are commanded "to love Hashem,"⁶ which means serv-

---

3. *Hilchot Teshuvah* 9:2.
4. *Avot* 1:3.
5. *Hilchot Teshuvah* 10:1–4.
6. Devarim 11:13.

ing Him out of love — implementing the truth because it is true, and the good will follow automatically; and because it is correct to serve the Master.

The *Mesilat Yesharim*,[7] too, seems to contradict himself. He says:[8] The intention that serving Hashem will purify our soul and enable us to enter Gan Eden is not bad, but it is self-serving. The best intention is to increase Hashem's glory.

How can we resolve the contradiction?

RESOLVING THE CONTRADICTION

Think of a student in yeshiva. Why is he studying Torah? Out of love for the Torah. At the same time, he must be careful to observe all the yeshiva's regulations so that he will not be evicted.

We must be careful not to lock ourselves out of Gan Eden by committing sins — especially those on our Sages' list of sins that exclude a person from Gan Eden, such as embarrassing someone in front of other people.[9] The fear of being left out should accompany us through life, as it did David, who said, "I know that the righteous have a share in the world to come, but I am afraid that sin may interfere."[10]

Thus *Mesilat Yesharim* begins by defining our goal as entering Gan Eden — because Hashem created us for this purpose; thus He commanded us to move toward it and make sure not to fall and find ourselves outside. But this is only the "foundation" and "root." There is more, as he explains later: Our intention should be to serve the Creator not to seek our own benefit, but out of love.

---

7. Ch. 19.
8. Ch. 19.
9. See Rambam, *Hilchot Teshuvah* 3:6–14.
10. *Berachot* 4a.

The Rambam[11] defines the ideal love of Hashem:

To love Hashem with an extremely great, powerful love until his soul is bound to love of Hashem, and he thinks about it always, as one who is lovesick.... As He commanded us, "with all your heart and with all your soul."

THE RAMBAM

As noted earlier, the Rambam tells us to serve Hashem not for the reward but rather out of love of Hashem, meaning because it is correct to serve the Master,[12] and also to implement the truth because it is true, and the good will follow automatically;[13]

We may understand these two points as follows.

Doing a mitzvah is powerful. Two of the things that it accomplishes are bringing satisfaction to Hashem by fulfilling His Will, as we say in *Leshem Yihud* before doing a mitzvah. This is what the Rambam means, that it is correct to serve the Master.

Fulfilling a mitzvah also draws us close to to our Creator, which is the ultimate truth, and it is delightful and pleasurable, as David testified: "As for me, closeness to Hashem is my good."[14] But there is self-interest here. Thus the Rambam says: Do not serve Hashem for this purpose, but implement the truth because it is true.

The *Ohr HaHayyim*[15] says that by doing a mitzvah the person makes himself a chariot for the Shechinah. And this is the secret of "I shall walk in your midst."[16]

---

11. *Hilchot Teshuvah* 10:3.
12. *Hilchot Teshuvah* 10:4.
13. *Hilchot Teshuvah* 10:2.
14. Tehilim 73:28.
15. Vayikra 18:4.
16. Vayikra 26:12.

PAYMENTS

We conclude with an interesting statement from *Midrash Tanhuma:*[17]

> The payment for a mitzvah is a mitzvah, and the payment for a sin is a sin.

Etz Yosef explains that receiving the reward of a mitzvah is itself a mitzvah; and receiving the punishment for a sin is itself a sin. How so?

Hashem created people in order to bestow good on them. So when we make this possible by doing a mitzvah, we are fulfilling His Will. On the other hand, when a person forces Hashem, as it were, to punish him by committing a sin, the punishment, too, is considered a sin.

Perhaps when we do a mitzvah and think of the reward, we should intend to fulfill Hashem's Will to bestow good on us.

---

17. Vayakhel 1.

PARASHAT

Kedoshim

DISGUSTED BY SIN

Kedoshim tehiyu, You shall be holy....[1]

What does the mitzvah to "be holy" entail?

Rashi explains: "Be separate from immorality and from sin, for wherever you find a fence against immorality, you find holiness."

But since immorality and sin are already forbidden, what is added by the mitzvah to be holy?

We can look for an answer in the verse "I have separated you from the nations to be Mine."[2] There Rashi[3] explains: Your separation from them should be for My sake, separating from the sin and accepting Hashem's Kingship. Don't say, "I can't bear to eat pork." Say, "I can, I certainly can, but the Torah forbids it."

That is only the first step, then comes the second step: to develop an aversion to pork. That is precisely the mitzvah of *Kedoshim tehiyu:* Separate yourself from anything the Torah forbids until you feel revolted by it.

It is known that we can wean ourselves of a harmful thing by

---

1. Vayikra 19:2.
2. Vayikra 20:26.
3. Citing out Sages.

convincing ourselves that it is disgusting. For instance, smokers who have persuaded themselves that cigarettes are disgusting become nauseated by the sight of one. The same applies to sin.

When a beautiful Roman noblewoman tried to lure Rabbi Akiva into sin, the sight of her so disgusted him that he spat on the floor.[4] On another occasion, he had to travel to a distant land, and its king sent beautiful women to accompany him. When the king asked him about his reaction, he replied, "What can I do? They were malodorous to me like rodents."[5]

And if someone started speaking *lashon hara* to the Hafetz Hayyim him, he would tremble.

This is the mitzvah of *Kedoshim tehiyu:* Separate yourself from immorality and sin to the point of having an aversion to them.

PLANTING TREES

וְכִי תָבֹאוּ אֶל הָאָרֶץ וּנְטַעְתֶּם כָּל עֵץ מַאֲכָל, And when you come to the Land, you shall plant every fruit tree. You shall treat its fruit as forbidden; for three years they shall be forbidden to you, they shall not be eaten....[6]

Why does our verse begin with "and"?[7]

In order to answer this question, let's first discuss the Midrash,[8] which quotes Hashem telling the Jewish people, "Although you will find the Land full of bounty, still you should plant fruit trees. Just as you entered and found trees that others had planted, so you should plant for your children."

---

4. *Nedarim* 50b, Rashi.
5. See *Avot d'Rabbi Natan,* ch. 16.
6. Vayikra 19:23.
7. Compare Vayikra 23:10: "When you come to the Land...," without "and."
8. *Tanhuma, ot* 8.

The Midrash illustrates with the story of the Roman king Hadrian, who once passed an old man planting fig trees. "You are old," said the king. "You are toiling for others!"

"Your majesty," replied the old man, "perhaps I will yet merit to eat of the fruits. But if I don't, my children will."

Three years later, the king again passed by the same place. The old man filled a basket with new figs, presented it to the king, and said, "Your majesty, I am the old man to whom you spoke. Hashem has allowed me to eat of the fruits that I planted, and here are some for you."

The king immediately ordered his servants to take the basket and fill it with gold coins, and the old man happily went home with the king's gift.

What does this story have to do with our verse?

Besides giving us the mitzvah of *orlah*[9] in our verse, the Torah is also commanding us to plant fruit trees, as the Midrash says. The Vilna Gaon said that each mitzvah is also a basic principle. If so, we must learn from the principle conveyed by the mitzvah of planting fruit trees to contribute something additional to our community for the benefit of the next generation. For instance, we might add *sefarim*,[10] benches, or a room to an existing synagogue.

And if we are obligated to contribute something constructive, certainly we are forbidden to do anything destructive! Vandalism is strictly prohibited. So is littering. Even if there is already litter on the floor or in the street, we must not add to it — especially in the Land of Israel, which was so beloved to our Sages that Rabbi Abba kissed the stones of Accre and Rabbi Hanina made repairs in his city.[11]

---

9. Treating the fruits of the first three years as forbidden.
10. Books.
11. *Ketubot* 112a.

It is told that a yeshiva student took a Mussar *sefer,* studied it for a while with great enthusiasm, and then went to the Mashgiah. "Rabbi," he said, "Mussar demands so much. Where should I begin?"

The Mashgiah replied, "Begin by returning the *sefer* to its place."

If causing disorder, dirt, or damage are forbidden in the physical and material realm, how much more so in the spiritual realm!

All of this is taught by the mitzvah "you shall plant every fruit tree."

AND BACK TO "AND"

Accordingly, we can understand why the verse begins with "And." "And" links the mitzvah of planting fruit trees to the rest of Parashat Kedoshim, which is mainly about the laws of *ben adam lehavero.*[12]

Thus the Parashah begins: "Speak to the entire congregation of the Children of Israel and say to them, *Kedoshim tehiyu.*" Rashi comments: This teaches that this Parashah was delivered in *hakhel*[13] because it contains most of the major laws of the Torah.

But how was this different than the rest of the Torah which was said in *Hakhel?*[14]

We may explain as follows.

With the rest of the Torah, Moshe stated each law publicly and then explained how to do it. For instance, he said, "You shall tie them as a sign on your hand" and then explained how to make tefillin and put them on. He said, "You shall write them on the

---

12. Interpersonal relationships.
13. In an assembly of the entire people.
14. The question is asked by Siftei Hachamim.

doorposts" and then explained how to make a mezuzah and put it up.

Parashat Kedoshim is different. It contains many mitzvot *ben adam lehavero,* and teaching them amounts to delivering rebuke. When a person in *hakhel* heard from Moshe that he must avoid causing the slightest unpleasantness to others, it was not theoretical "others"; he probably thought about the friend standing next to him. Thus the *hakhel* here made the rebuke more beneficial.

SEQUEL TO THE STORY

The Midrash about the old man and the fig trees continues: A neighboring woman who overheard the exchange with the king advised that her husband also bring the king a basket of fruit. The husband did as advised, but instead of gold, he received a beating. The Midrash concludes that bad wives bring troubles upon their husbands.

Why does the Midrash need to tell us about the woman who gave her husband bad advice? What does it have to do with the mitzvah of planting fruit trees?

As we have seen, from this mitzvah we learn to refrain from anything destructive. This woman gave her husband bad advice out of jealousy, thereby causing him harm.

Bad midot and sins are destructive. They ruin the beautiful world that Hashem created, as it is written, "Your trangressions have overturned these [blessings], and your sins have kept goodness away from you;"[15] and, "A fruitful land [is turned] into a salty waste because of the wickedness of its inhabitants."[16]

---

15. Yirmiyahu 5:25.
16. Tehilim 107:34. See also *Ketubot* 112b.

Small wonder that when Hashem created Adam, He took him around to all the trees of Gan Eden and told him, "See how wonderful My creations are. And whatever I created, I created for you. Be careful lest you sin and destroy My world."[17]

Mesilat Yesharim[18] explains: The world was created for the use of man. But if a person is drawn after the world [that is, worldly desires and pleasures] and distances himself from his Creator, he ruins himself, and the world together with him.

Our Sages, in the Midrash,[19] wanting to teach people that sin ruins the world, told the following: In the good times of Shimon ben Shetah and Queen Shelom-Tzion, they stored away samples of the blessed produce for future generations. For in those days, rain would fall on Shabbat evenings [so as not to disturbe people's work]; and the wheat became like kidneys, the barley like olive pits, and the lentils like gold coins.

ALL-INCLUSIVE

Ve'ahavta lere'acha kamocha, You shall love your neighbor as yourself.[20]

Says the Sifra: Rabbi Akiva called, "You shall love your neighbor as yourself," a great principle (*klal*) of the Torah. Ben Azai said: "This is the book of man's generations"[21] is an even greater one.

Klal comes from the root "include." Rabbi Akiva called this mitzvah a principle that includes the whole Torah. Why? And why did Ben Azai say that the other verse is an even greater one?

---

17. *Midrash Kohelet* 7:13.
18. Chapter 1.
19. *Vayikra Rabbah* 35:9.
20. Vayikra 19:18.
21. Bereshit 5:1.

A similar question may be asked about Rabban Yohanan ben Zakai,[22] who told his five disciples to figure out what evil path a person should stay far away from — that is, what one thing can lead to abandoning the whole Torah.

Four of the answers — a bad eye, a wicked friend, a wicked neighbor, an evil heart — are understandable. But Rabbi Shimon's answer — one who borrows and does not repay — is not. It seems that the borrower sinned only against one person, the lender, why should this lead to abandoning the whole Torah?

We may answer in light of a statement ascribed to Rabbi Shimon Shkop *zt"l*: If a person looks down on his friends, he cannot be humble vis-à-vis Hashem.

In other words, a person must work on the *ben adam lehavero* mitzvot and thereby acquire good *midot*.[23] Then he will be able activitate those *midot* vis-à-vis Hashem.

The *midah* of gratitude, in particular, is fundamental to mitzvah observance. Hashem says to us, "Who built a guardrail on his roof before I gave him a house? Who put tzitzit on his garment before I gave him a garment? Who circumcised his son before I gave him a son?"[24]

A borrower who does not repay a loan is demonstrating a lack of gratitude toward the lender. If he has no gratitude in him, he cannot activate this *midah* to serve Hashem. Thus failing to repay a loan is an evil path that affects the observance of all other mitzvot.

The same applies to loving your neighbor. Only if we have love in us can we activate this *midah* to serve Hashem. A person who does not love his fellow men cannot love Hashem.

This explains the famous story of the gentile who wished to

---

22. See *Avot* 2:14.
23. Character traits.
24. As our Sages expound the verse *Mi hikdimani va'ashalem* (Iyov 41:3).

convert but wanted to be taught the whole Torah on one foot. The gentile wanted to focus on one principle that influences all mitzvah observance. Hillel told him to focus on loving *re'acha* (your neighbor/friend/fellow). Rashi says that in this way he would reach love of Hashem, Who is called *re'acha* in the verse "Forsake not your friend (*re'acha*) and the friend of your father."[25] And this, in turn, would lead to keeping all the mitzvot.

So Rabbi Akiva called "You shall love your neighbor as yourself"[26] a great, all-inclusive principle of the Torah.

Ben Azai said that there is an even greater one — to always keep in mind that we are writing a book, as our Sages taught: "All your deeds are being recorded in a book."[27] Says Hovot Ha-Levavot:[28] Your days are pages, on which you can write what you would like to have read about you in the world to come. That is, this permanent record of our deeds, good and otherwise, and how we kept mitzvoth, will be open for all to read in the world to come.

This awareness is vital to the success of our mission in this world. That is why Ben Azai called it a greater all-inclusive principle than loving your neighbor.

New acquaintances are often asked, "What do you do?" There is one answer that holds true for us all: I'm writing a book. When will it come out? In the world to come.

---

25. Mishlei 27:10.
26. Vayikra 19:18.
27. *Avot* 2:1.
28. *Shaar Heshbon HaNefesh,* ch. 3.

PARASHAT

Emor

COUNTING THE OMER

You shall count for yourselves... seven weeks.[1]

Says the Gemara:[2]

Rabbi Akiva had twelve thousand pairs of disciples from Gevet to Antipras..., and they all died between Pesach and Shavuot because *lo nahagu kavod zeh lazeh* [generally translated: they did not treat each other with respect]. And the world was desolate [for the Torah was forgotten[3]] until Rabbi Akiva went to [five] Sages in the south and taught it to them.... And they established the Torah at that time.

Several questions arise here:

- ◈ Why does it say "twelve thousand pairs of students" rather than "twenty-four thousand students"?
- ◈ Why did they die between Pesach and Shavuot?
- ◈ Why does it say, *zeh lazeh,* literally: "one to the other"? In Hebrew, the normal expression for showing respect goes with *zeh bazeh,* "one with the other."

---

1. Vayikra 23:15.
2. *Yevamot* 62b.
3. Rashi.

◆ Since when is not treating one another with sufficient respect a capital offense?

◆ Why was the world "desolate"? There were many other Sages, such as Rabbi Yishmael, Rabbi Yehoshua, the disciples of the schools of Hillel and Shammai and others.

◆ Why did our Sages ordain mourning for all generations over the death of these 24,000, when we lost millions of Jews in other calamaties?

Clues to the answer are found in the Midrash.[4]

> Rabbi Akiva said: I had twenty-four thousand disciples, and all of them died during my lifetime between Pesach and Shavuot. Eventually, seven were raised up for me.... I said to them, "The first ones died only because they were begrudging toward one another in Torah. Don't you be like that!" Immediately they arose and filled the entire Land of Israel with Torah.

Accordingly, the reason they died was not lack of respect, but because they did not want to pass on their knowledge to other disciples. Most likely, Rabbi Akiva did not learn with them all simultaneously; rather he taught different tractates to different groups with the expectation that they would then teach one another. Instead, each disciple learned only with his own study partner, and they became twelve thousand pairs of disciple.

Thus the Gemara says, *lo nahagu kavod zeh lazeh.* "Honor" is Torah. They did not want to give this honor to others.

In every generation Hashem plants a Torah giant whose mission is to disseminate Torah among the Jewish people. Examples are Rabbi Yehudah HaNassi, who redacted the Mishnah, and

---

4. Kohelet 11:6.

Ravina and Rav Ashi, who redacted the Gemara. An example in modern times is my teacher Rabbi Aharon Kotler *zt"l*, who built up Torah in America.

The Gemara[5] says that Moshe Rabbenu was shown Rabbi Akiva, and his reaction was, "You have such a man in Your world, and You are giving the Torah through me?!" This shows that Rabbi Akiva had the ability and the mission of giving Torah to the Jewish people.

Evidently, out of the many Sages at the time, Rabbi Akiva was the one designated by heaven to raise disciples who would transmit the Torah to the coming generations. Thus he planned for his disciples to spread throughout the Land of Israel and teach the people Torah. But since they did not transmit their knowledge to one another, their Torah knowledge was incomplete and could not be spread. That is why Hashem took them from this world. Then Rabbi Akiva went to the south and raised up five (or seven) disciples who undertook to transmit the complete Torah in the Land of Israel.

It is significant that the deaths occurred in the period between Pesach and Shavuot. Rabbi Aaron Kotler[6] explains that during this period, we prepare ourselves to receive the Torah by strengthening ourselves in the forty-eight ways that the Torah is acquired.[7] These include closeness with colleagues, a good heart, and sharing the yoke of one's friend. Included also is *machri'o lekaf zechut*, which is generally understood as giving him the benefit of the doubt and judging him favorably. But literally, it may be translated "tilting him to the side of privilege" — giving him the privilege of knowing what you know.

We mourn during this period because had those twenty-four

---

5. *Menahot* 29b.
6. *Mishnat Rabbi Aharon.*
7. See *Avot* 6:6.

thousand disciples taught Torah, there would have been much more Torah in the world. With more Jews throughout the generations knowing more Torah, our nation would have been protected from assimilation and from holocausts.

LAG BA'OMER

The *Shulhan Aruch*[8] says that the twenty-four thousand disciples whom Rabbi Akiva taught in his youth stopped dying on Lag Ba'Omer.[9] This is the day of the death of Rabbi Shimon bar Yohai, author of the *Zohar* and one of the handful of disciples whom Rabbi Akiva taught in his old age. Let's examine the Gemara that relates the story of Rabbi Shimon.[10]

> Rabbi Yehudah said, "How fine are the works of this people [the Romans]! They have made markets, built bridges, and erected baths."
>
> Rabbi Shimon said, "All that they did was for themselves. They made markets to set harlots in them; baths, to rejuvenate themselves; bridges, to levy tolls from them."

Let's compare this to a different Talmudic passage:[11]

> In Days to Come, Hashem will bring the Torah Scroll... and announce, "Let whoever occupied himself with it come and take his reward."
>
> ...Immediately, the kingdom of Rome will come before Him.... Hashem will ask them, "What did you occupy yourselves with?"
>
> "Master of the world," they will say..., "we built many markets, we made many bathhouses, we increased silver and gold — and

---

8. *Siman* 493.
9. The thiry-third day of the Omer.
10. *Shabbat* 33b.
11. *Avodah Zarah* 2b.

everything that we did was only so that the Jewish people could study Torah."

Hashem will tell them, "Fools...! All that you did was only for yourselves. You made markets to set harlots in them; baths, to rejuvenate yourselves. And the gold and silver is mine."

...The Roman kingdom will leave, and the Persian will enter....

Accordingly, the discussion between Rabbi Yehudah and Rabbi Shimon parallels the discussion between the Romans and Hashem. Why did Rabbi Yehudah praise them for what Hashem will call them fools?

Because their argument is correct, and they truly deserve reward for what they did.

If a coin falls out of our pocket and a pauper finds it and uses it to feed his family, we are accredited with giving charity. Bottom line, the pauper benefited, regardless of our lack of intention.

The Romans and other gentile nations will claim that they deserve a reward, regardless of their intentions. For they built bridges, which enabled yeshiva students to travel to yeshiva; and today, they build airplanes that transport boys to yeshivot far from home, as a result of which Torah study flourishes. This is just one example of how Jews benefit from things that the gentiles do.

If so, why will Hashem call them fools?

Of the Torah it is written, 'Length of days is in her right; in her left are wealth and glory."[12] Our Sages[13] explained: For those who occupy themselves with Torah for pure motives, there is length of days in the world to come. But for those who do so for other motives, there is wealth and glory in this world, but no reward in the world to come.

---

12. Mishlei 3:16.
13. *Shabbat* 63a.

In the course of world history, the gentiles have received a great deal of wealth and glory. This was their reward for benefitting the Jews unintentionally. But they are not entitled to reward in the world to come.

Thus Rabbi Yehudah's praised deeds for which the gentiles receive reward in this world. But Rabbi Shimon was referring to the world to come, from which they are excluded because their intentions were selfish.

THE CAVE

The Gemara goes on to relate that the Roman rulers of the Land of Israel heard what Rabbi Shimon had said, and they wanted him killed. Rabbi Shimon fled with his son Rabbi Elazar to a cave, where they studied Torah while sitting up to their necks in sand and subsisting on carobs and water. Only after twelve years did they come out. Then:

> Seeing a man plowing and sowing, they exclaimed, "They forsake eternal life and engage in temporal life!" Whatever they fixed their eyes on was immediately burnt up.

Surely these great Sages did not burn grain — we are forbidden to destroy anything useful or to cause people any damage! Evidently what they burned was straw and stubble. Their purpose was to show people the uselessness of devoting themselves to this world, for in the end it will all go up in smoke.

> Thereupon a heavenly voice rang out and said, "Have you emerged to destroy My world? Return to your cave!"
> They returned and dwelt there twelve months....Then they came out....
> On Erev Shabbat before sunset, they saw an old man holding two bundles of [fragrant] myrtle branches and running....

"What are these for?" they asked him.

"They are in honor of Shabbat," he replied....

"See how precious the mitzvot are to Jews!" Rabbi Shimon told his son, and their minds were set at ease.

Why were their minds set at ease?

They saw the old man running to disconnect himself from this-worldly occupations and enter the world of Shabbat, which is a semblance of the world to come — it reflects the situation we will face there. For on Shabbat we have only what we prepare beforehand. If we don't prepare light, we will sit in the dark; if we don't prepare food, we will go hungry; and if we prepare a meager meal, we will have little to eat. In the world to come, too, we will have only the "lamp of mitzvah and the light of Torah" that we prepared here. And the more we invest in the quality of a mitzvah here, the more the mitzvah will glow and flourish there.

They also saw the fragrant myrtle branches, and perceived that even while toiling in this world, a Jew sets his sights toward the world of souls. For fragrance delights the soul, as the Gemara[14] states; and the old man took the branches in order to recite the blessing over fragrance and smell them.

The Gemara continues:

Rabbi Pinhas ben Yair, the son-in-law of Rabbi Shimon, heard and went out to meet him. He took him into the baths and massaged his skin. Seeing the clefts in his body [caused by sitting buried in sand for thirteen years], Rabbi Pinhas wept. The tears streamed from his eyes and entered the cracks in the skin, and Rabbi Shimon cried out [in pain].

"Woe to me that I see you thus!" said Rabbi Pinhas.

---

14. *Berachot* 43b.

That is, out of distress over your suffering, the tears fell by themselves and entered the cracks in your skin.

> "Happy are you that you see me thus," said Rabbi Shimon, "for if you did not see me thus [afflicted] you would not find me thus [learned]."

We would have expected Rabbi Shimon to say, "Happy am I that you see me thus." Why did he say, "Happy are you"?

We may answer in light of Rabbi Yehudah HaNassi's statement: "The reason I am sharper than my colleagues is that I saw Rabbi Meir from the back. Had I seen him from the front, I would have been even sharper!"[15]

What we see has an impact on us. On the negative side, our Sages told us that a man who sees a *sotah*[16] in her disgrace should abstain from wine. Seeing a decline in Jewish purity has a negative effect on the viewer.

However, seeing a tzaddik elevates the viewer, surely if the tzaddik separated himself from worldly life, toiled in Torah while suffering, and ascended immeasurably from it. Such was Rabbi Shimon, of whom we sing, "In a rocky cave where you stayed, you acquired your majesty and glory." Seeing Rabbi Shimon would surely draw down sanctity and purity on Rabbi Pinhas, who should therefore be happy.

SHAVUOT AND FOOD

[On Shavuot,] you shall offer a new meal-offering to Hashem.[17]

---

15. *Eruvin* 13b.
16. Wayward wife.
17. Vayikra 23:16.

Much of Parashat Emor is devoted to the festivals, which are times of joy for us. Our Sages[18] are divided about what must be done at these times.

Rabbi Eliezer said: On Yom Tov, a person either eats and drinks or else sits and learns.

Rabbi Yehoshua said: Split the day, half for Hashem [e.g., learning] and half for you [e.g., eating a festive meal].

And both Sages based themselves on the same verse.

But all agree that on Shavuot, "for you" is also required. Why? Because it is the day on which the Torah was given to the Jewish people.

Why must the day of the giving of the Torah be celebrated with a festive meal?

Rabbi Eliyahu Lopian answers that we are required to eat on Shavuot because we must sanctify the physical aspect of life through the ways of Torah.

Bet HaLevi answers that when Moshe Rabbenu went up to heaven to bring down the Torah, the angels objected claimng that it should stay in heaven, with them. Moshe's argument that only men can fulfill mitzvot that are connected to physical things convinced them. Therefore on Shavuot, we must eat and fulfill the mitzvot that are connected to food.

Now we understand why eating is required. But why a festive meal?

We may answer in light of the Gemara's[19] statement that Ahav king of Israel enticed Yehoshafat king of Judah to join him in battle through a good meal, as it is written,[20] "Ahav slaughtered

---

18. *Pesahim* 68b.
19. *Hullin* 4b.
20. Divrei HaYamim 2 18:2.

abundant sheep and cattle for him [Yehoshafat] and the people accompanying him, and he enticed him to go to war against Ramot Gilad."

This is human nature, which Hashem implanted in us. If someone serves us a good meal, we tend to be amenable to the host's proposals.

Rabbi Dessler *zt"l* taught that on every holiday, the same spiritual light that originally shone on that day shines today as well. On Shavuot, Hashem offers us the Torah. In order to accept it willingly and joyfully, we eat from Hashem's table.

Rashi[21] makes an additional point:

> A person should rejoice on [this day] with a festve meal, to show that the Jewish people are pleased with this day, on which the Torah was given.

Thus Rav Yosef asked his family to prepare him a special calf, "for if not for this day, how many Yosefs are there in the marketplace!"

Accordingly, the Shavuot meal is a *se'udat hodayah*, a meal of thanksgiving. This explains why even Rabbi Eliezer, who maintains that a festive meal is not obligatory on Pesach or Sukot, agrees that it is obligatory on Shavuot — just as it is on the occasion of a wedding or a circumcision, which are meals of thanksgiving to the Creator that cannot be replaced with Torah study. With the Shavuot meal, we thank Hashem for His wonderful Torah, which transforms our life.

---

21. On *Pesahim* 68b.

PEACE

When you reap the harvest of your land, do not completely remove the corners of your field as you reap, and do not gather the gleaning of your harvest. For the poor and the convert shall you leave them....[22]

Why are the laws of *pe'ah* and *leket* sandwiched between the laws of the holidays and their respective sacrfices?

Rashi asks this question, and he answers: To teach you that whoever gives these gifts to the poor, properly, is considered as if he built the Temple and offered sacrifices in it.

Why? What does caring for the poor have in common with offering sacrfices?

We may answer in light of the Midrash[23] that states: Hashem says, as it were, "This pauper was complaining, 'How am I different from So-and-So? Why does he sleep on a comfortable bed in a nice house, while I...!' When you give charity to him, I consider it as if you made peace between him and Me." Thus it is written, "...he will make peace for Me."[24]

Just as giving charity restores the peace between Hashem and His children, so does bringing sacrifices — not only the peace offerings, but also the offerings that atone for sin.

Thus, regarding the mitzvah of rejoicing on the festivals, the Rambam[25] rules:

When a man eats and drinks, he is required to feed converts, orphans, widows, and other unfortunate poor people. If instead he locks his doors and eats and drinks only with his children and his

22. Vayikra 23:22.
23. *Vayikra Rabbah* 34:16.
24. Yeshayahu 27:5.
25. *Hilchot Yom Tov* 6:18.

wife, without giving food and drink to the poor and miserable, this is not the joy of a mitzvah, but the joy of his stomach.

SUKKOT AND KNOWLEDGE

In sukkot shall you dwell for seven days... so that your generations will know that I caused the Children of Israel to dwell in sukkot when I took them out of the land of Egypt....[26]

The Torah tells us to dwell in sukkot "so that your generations will know...," whereas concerning the matzot we eat on Pesach the Torah tells us, "so that you will remember the day of your departure from the land of Egypt."[27] Why is the language different?

In order to answer the question, let's first analyze those sukkot in the desert. What exactly were they?

The Midrash[28] presents two opinions. Rabbi Akiva says that Hashem made them actual sukkot. Others say that these sukkot refer to the clouds of glory in which He enveloped the Jewish camp, as described in Tehilim,[29] "He spread out a cloud for shelter."

The Midrash continues: These cloud of glory were in the desert. How do we know that He did the same in the Land? From the verse "In sukkot shall you dwell for seven days." How do we know that he will do the same in Days to Come? From the verse "There will be a sukkah as a shade from heat in the daytime, as a protection and refuge from storm and from rain."[30]

Accordingly, the sukkot that we build today take the place of the clouds of glory that enveloped us in the desert. Our sukkot are

---

26. Vayikra 23:42.
27. Devarim 16:3.
28. *Yalkut Shimoni, Emor* 655.
29. Tehilim 105:39.
30. Yeshayahu 4:6.

not a mere remembrance but rather a continuation of those protective clouds. That is why a flimsy sukkah can protect and save, so that before retiring for the night in the sukkah it is not necessary to say the usual verses of protection. When we sit in a sukkah, we are experiencing envelopment in Hashem's cloud.

Eating matzah, in contrast, reminds us of the past — of what our ancestors ate in Egypt. Therefore it says, "so that you will remember."

In light of this, we can answer another question.

The clouds of glory were only one of three wonderful gifts that Hashem gave the Jewish people in the desert. In the merit of Aharon, Moshe, and Miriam, He gave them the clouds, the manna, and the traveling well, respectively. Why do we commemorate only the clouds, but not the manna or the well?

Because the point is not to remember, but to experience what was in the desert in order to bring ourselves closer to perfection.

Now we can also understand the opinion of Rabbi Akiva: Hashem made our ancestors sukkot, housing that is small and temporary, while they were wandering from place to place. When we sit in a sukkah, we experience and know what they learned then — tolerance for one another, which is essential when living together in a small space. As the saying goes, when there is room in the heart, there is room in the house.

Such a teaching is characteristic of Rabbi Akiva, who taught that "Love your neighbor like yourself" is a great underlying principle of the Torah.

PARASHAT

Behar

BITAHON

Six years shall you sow your field... and you shall gather its crop. But the seventh year... you shall not sow your field....[1]

Compare:

Six days shall you work... but the seventh day is Shabbat; you shall do not work...."[2]

When commanding us to let the land rest during the Shemitah year, why does the Torah tell us to sow our field for six years? And when commanding us to rest on Shabbat, why does the Torah tell us to work for six days?

We may answer that Shemitah and Shabbat teach us *bitahon*, trusting that everything is from Hashem. On both the seventh day of the week and the seventh year, Hashem sustains us without any effort on our part. From this we should come to understand that during the preceding six years or days, it is also only Hashem Who sustains us. The reason we toil is only to fulfill the decree of "By

---

1. Vayikra 25:3–4.
2. Shemot 20:9–10.

the sweat of your brow shall you eat bread."[3] This point is made by the verse "Six days work shall be done"[4] — as if the work is accomplished by itself, without any worldly exertion on our part.

Where our exertion does matter is only in prayer — and not only when we feel a lack. In times of plenty as in times of hunger, it is only Hashem Who sustains us, and He does so always. As we say in the Nishmat prayer, "In hunger You nourished us, and in plenty You sustained is."

Even if our pantry is well stocked, says the *Zohar*,[5] we should ask Hashem for food every day, in order to bring down blessing. Rabbi Yisa Sabba would always pray for food before preparing his daily meal. For he said, "We will not prepare a meal until it is given by the King." After praying, he would wait an hour, like someone who has made a request and is waiting for it to be granted.

Now we can understand why the morning blessings and the Amidah are in the present tense. When we say *pokeah ivrim,* "Who gives sight to the blind," we should think, "Right now, Hashem is opening my eyes." When we say, *honen hadaat,* "Who grants knowledge," we should think, "Right now, Hashem is granting me knowledge." And so on for each blessing.

We should always feel that right now, Hashem is giving us what we need — because in fact He is doing just that.

ACTS OF KINDNESS

If your brother becomes impoverished... you shall strengthen him....[6]

---

3. Bereshit 3:19.
4. Shemot 35:2.
5. *Beshalah* 62a.
6. Vayikra 25:25

How are we to "strengthen him"?

There are two ways: one is with money; the other is with encouraging words. Says the Gemara:[7] Whoever gives a needy person money with which he can buy food is blessed with six blessings, listed in the passage[8] "Break your bread for the hungry.... Then your light will burst out like the dawn...."[9] But whoever appeases him is blessed with eleven blessings, listed in the continuation:[10] "Offer your soul to the hungry and satisfy the afflicted soul. Then your light will shine in the darkness...."[11]

And if someone both appeases the needy person and gives him money, it is clear from the Gemara and Tosafot that he receives both sets of blessings, a grand total of seventeen.

Even if a person has no money to give, he can still "offer his soul to the hungry" — by telling him, "My soul goes out to you." The very fact that someone shares his distress "satisfies the afflicted soul" soothing him so that he becomes at peace with Hashem,[12] with the world, and with himself. And peace is equivalent to all other blessings combined.[13]

The opposite side of the coin is that inflicting pain with words

---

7. *Bava Batra* 9b.

8. Yeshayahu 58:7–9.

9. "...[1] your light will burst out like the dawn, and [2] your healing will speedily sprout; [3] your righteous deed will precede you, and [4] the glory of Hashem will gather you in. Then [5] you will call and Hashem will respond; [6] you will cry out and He will say, 'Here I am!'"

10. Yeshayahu 58:10–12.

11. "...your light will shine in the darkness, and your deepest gloom will be like the noon. Then Hashem will guide you always, sate your soul in times of drought and strengthen your bones; and you will be like a well-watered garden and a spring of water whose water never fail. Ancient ruins wil be rebuilt through you, and you will restore generations-old foundations; and they will call you, 'reparer of the reach' and 'restorer of paths for habitation.'"

12. See "Peace" in "Parashat Emor."

13. Rashi, Vayikra 26:6.

is worse than robbery, as the Gemara[14] teaches. For painful words rob the victim of his joy of life and peace of mind, which is worse than robbing him of his money. Besides, money can be returned, but the harm caused by painful words lasts forever.

THE *PARITZ*[15] AND THE JEW

Practically speaking, how is it possible to comfort a person in distress?

The Hafetz Hayyim answers with a parable:

A *paritz* had a faithful Jewish tenant who always paid his rent on time. One day the landowner decided to go away for a year, and he appointed a manager in his absence. The manager raised the Jew's rent and warned that he would be punished with a lashing every day he was late paying. The Jew was unable to pay the high rent on time, and in the course of the year he received fifty lashings.

When the *paritz* returned, the Jew told him how he had been treated. The *paritz* immediately summoned the manager and said. "For each lashing you gave the Jew, pay him a thousand rubles!"

The Jew hurried home to share the good news with his wife. Then he added wistfully, "Too bad he gave me only fifty lashings! If only he had given me a hundred..."

When a person arrives in the world to come and sees the reward for his suffering, he, too, will say, "If only I had suffered more...."

HLLEL'S KINDNESS

If your brother becomes impoverished....[16]

---

14. *Bava Metzia* 59b.
15. Polish landowner.
16. Vayikra 25:25

On our verse, the Midrash[17] says:

"A man of kindness does good for himself."[18] This refers to Hillel the Elder. When he parted with his disciples and began to go, they asked him, "Rabbi, where are you going?"

He replied, "To do a mitzvah."

"Which mitzvah?" they asked.

"To bathe in the bathhouse," he replied.

"Is that a mitzvah?" they asked.

He replied, "Yes. If someone who is in charge of a statue of the king washes it.... how much more so I, who have been created in the image of G-d [should make sure that I keep clean]!"

The Midrash continues:

"A man of kindness does good for himself" refers to Hillel the Elder. When he parted with his disciples and began to go, they asked him, "Rabbi, where are you going?"

He replied, "To do *hesed*[19] for a guest in my house.

"Do you have a guest every day?" they asked.

He replied, "Is the soul not a guest in my body? Today it is here; tomorrow, it isn't."

Why does the Midrash record these anecdotes about Hillel in connection with the verse "If your brother becomes impoverished"?

We can answer in light of the Gemara's[20] discussion of the few mitzvot whose dividends a person enjoys in this world while the principal remains intact for him in the world to come. The Gemara counts praying with *kavanah*[21] as *hesed* and Rashi writes that the

---

17. *Vayikra Rabbah* 34:3.
18. Mishlei 11:17.
19. Kindness.
20. Shabbat 127a; see Rashi.
21. Intent.

proof of this is from the verse, "A man of kindness does good for himself."

In other words, through prayer, we take care of our needs, and this is considered doing *hesed* for a needy Jew. "Your brother who becomes impoverished" includes ourselves! Resources come from Hashem, and He puts us in charge of distributing them to those in need, ourselves included.

Similarly, Rabbi Shalom Shwadron *zt"l* would say that when caring for our own children, we should think of ourself as caring for fellow Jews.

We can take this concept one step further.

Suppose we are downcast. Then we study Mussar (such as *Hovot HaLevavot*) about appreciating the wonderful kindnesses that Hashem bestows on us. As a result, our spirits are raised.

Since whoever raises the spirits of a downcast person is blessed with eleven blessings, we receive eleven blessings for strengthening ourselves!

PARASHAT
Behukotai

TOILING IN TORAH

Im behukotai telechu, If you will walk in My decrees and keep My mitzvot and do them ...[1]

What does this mean?

Says Rashi: "If you will walk in My decrees" cannot mean fulfillment of mitzvot; that is covered by "keep my mitzvot." Rather, it means: Always be toiling in Torah.

But Rashi continues: "And keep My mitzvot" — Always be toiling in Torah in order to keep [the prohibitions] and do [the positive commands], as in "You shall learn them and be careful to do them" (*ushemartem laasotam*).[2]

The two parts of Rashi don't jibe. According to the first part, the verse is about the lofty level of learning Torah and doing mitzvot with "toil" — amidst hardships. According to the second part, the verse is about learning in order to fulfill, which is the minimal level; a person who learns Torah without the intention of fulfilling what he learns is simply wicked.

The contradiction is resolved if we explain "Always be toiling in Torah" as follows:

---

1. Vayikra 26:3.
2. Devarim 5:1.

When learning about a mitzvah, prepare yourself to fulfill it. How? By picturing yourself as being in a situation where it is applicable.

In addition, when learning about a mitzvah, long to fulfill it, as the *Hayyei Adam*[3] deduces from *Ushemartem laasotam*. Although commonly translated "you shall be careful to do them," it also means "you shall wait eagerly to do them," as when Yaakov awaited (*shamar*) the fulfillment of Yosef's dreams.[4] Here we are commanded to look forward to mitzvot coming our way so that we can fulfill them.

For instance, suppose we learn that anger is forbidden, while forbearance is an important virtue. We should imagine an irritating situation and picture ourselves handling it calmly. Then, when we are challenged in real life, we will be able to exercise forbearance.

The classic example is the episode of Hillel on Erev Shabbat, when someone deliberately kept disturbing him with ridiculous questions. How was Hillel able to remain calm, polite, and even friendly toward this man? Evidently Hillel had prepared himself for the mitzvah.

Rabbi Akiva explicitly said that he used this technique. The Gemara[5] relates that while the Sage's flesh was being combed with iron, he said the Shema with *kavanah* and with joy. His disciples asked him how this was possible. He replied, "All my days I waited to fulfill the verse 'You shall love Hashem... with all your soul' — even if He takes your soul."

Advance preparation allowed Rabbi Akiva to withstand this

---

3. 68:15.
4. Bereshit 37:11.
5. End of *Berachot*.

trial. In this he resembled Avraham Avinu, who "walked before"[6] Hashem — as Hashem commanded Him, saying, "Walk before Me"[7] — and withstood ten trials.

Thus our verse says, *Im behukotai telechu,* "If you will walk in My decrees." The root *hok,* "decree," is related to *hakak,* "engrave." Hashem is telling us: Through the toil of review, yearning, and preparation, engrave the Torah in your hearts like Avraham, who walked before Me.

Hashem promises us that if we do so, "I will walk among you."[8] Rashi explains this as referring to the reward of Gan Eden.

When we reach the world to come and hope to be shown to Gan Eden, first we will have a test. Hashem will open the *Shulhan Aruch,* go through paragraph after paragraph, and ask us how we kept each mitzvah.

Rabbi Eliyahu Lopian was very particular to rise "like a lion" in the morning. Why? He explained that this is the first mitzvah in the *Shulhan Aruch,* and he wanted to spare himself the embarrassment of failing the test right at the start....

NAHUM ISH GAMZU

...I will not reject you [literally: I will not be revolted by you].[9]

The Gemara[10] tells us about the teacher of Rabbi Akiva:

Nahum Ish Gamzu was blind in both eyes, crippled in both hands, lame in both legs, and his whole body was covered with boils. He

---

6. See Bereshit 24:40.
7. Bereshit 17:1. See "The Tenth Trial" in "Parashat Vayera."
8. Vayikra 26:12.
9. Vayikra 26:11.
10. *Taʾanit* 21a.

lay in bed in a tottering house, with the legs of his bed standing in buckets of water to prevent worms from reaching his body.

His disciples wanted to remove his bed and then his belongings. "My children," he said, "first remove my belongings..., for... as long as I am in the house, the house will not collapse."

They removed his belongings and afterward his bed. Then the house collapsed.

"Our teacher," said his disciples, "since you are perfectly righteous, why did this befall you?"

"My children," he replied, "I brought it on myself.

"Once I was traveling on the road to my father-in-law's house, and I had with me three laden donkeys: one with food, one with drink, and one with various delicacies. A poor man approached me on the road and said, 'Rabbi, sustain me!'"

"I said to him, 'Wait and I will unload my donkey.'

"Before I managed to unload the donkey, his soul departed.

"I... fell on his face and said, 'Let my eyes, which did not have mercy on your eyes, go blind! Let my hands, which did not have mercy on your hands, become crippled! Let my feet, which did not have mercy on your feet, become lame.' I was not satisfied until I had said, 'Let my entire body become covered with boils.'"

Why did Nahum feel so guilty? Why did he think that he deserved such terrible suffering? He had told the pauper that he would unload the donkey and bring him food. What more could he have done?

We may answer in light of the *Talmud Yerushalmi's*[11] version of the episode, which adds two more details: The pauper was afflicted with boils; and Nahum told him, "Wait until I go to my father-in-law's house and unload the donkeys."

Apparently, everyone was revolted by the sight of this pauper

---

11. *Shekalim* 5:4.

and his boils. He hoped that at least this tzaddik would not loathe him.

But Nahum said he would unload the donkeys in his father-in-law's house. The pauper understood that Nahum would not unload them in his presence because he could not bear to be near him for even such a short time. The pain of rejection caused the pauper to die of sorrow.

To atone for this, Nahum invoked afflictions such that even the *hevra kadisha* would find it revolting to tend to his corpse. These measure-for-measure afflictions included repulsive boils. Out of respect for the tzaddik, the *Talmud Bavli* makes no mention of the pauper's boils; it leaves it to us to understand by ourselves.

In a similar vein, the Gemara[12] relates that Rabbi Elazer once encountered an extremely ugly man and asked him, "Are all the people of your town as ugly as you?"

"I don't know," replied the man, "but go and tell the Artisan who made me, 'How ugly is the vessel that you made!'"

At that, Rabbi Eliezer dismounted, prostrated himself before the man, and pleaded for forgiveness.

Thus we are forbidden to regard any Jew with disgust. The Hazon Ish *zt"l* fulfilled this teaching. He took care of a sick man who was unable to tend to his own bodily needs, and was not disgusted by him.

The *Yerushalmi* continues:

Rabbi Akiva said to his teacher, Nahum Ish Gamzu, "Alas for me that I see you this way."

Nahum replied, "Alas for me had you not seen yourself this way."

"Rabbi," said Rabbi Akiva, "are you cursing me?"

Nahum replied, "Are you rejecting afflictions?"

---

12. *Ta'anit* 19a.

Nahum was telling Rabbi Akiva: I fell short of the level of Avraham, who prepared himself in advance for trials. Had I prepared myself to never reject a Jew, I would not have been revolted; then I would have immediately unloaded the donkeys and given him food. Do not make the same mistake! Prepare yourself to fulfill mitzvot in any situation that may come your way.

Indeed, Rabbi Akiva followed his teacher's instructions, as he testified, "All my days I waited to fulfill the verse 'You shall love Hashem… with all your soul' — even if He takes your soul."

HUMASH
Bamidbar

PARASHAT

Bamidbar

GRAB THE OPPORTUNITY

Hashem spoke to Moshe in the Sinai desert..., saying:[1]

With this verse, the Torah begins Bamidbar, which is also known as the Humash of *Pekudim*, "Counting" or "Numbers." On this verse, Rashi comments:

> Because they [the children of Israel] are cherished by Him, He counts them at all times. When they went out of Egypt, He counted them. When they fell after the [sin of the golden] calf, He counted them to know how many were left. And [now,] when He came to rest His presence on them, He counted them.

But the Torah does not mention counting until the second verse: "*Se'u et rosh,* Take a census...."[2] Why didn't Rashi put his comment there?

And another question: Rashi says that the Jewish people are counted because Hashem cherishes them. But this seems to contradict a verse from the Haftarah:

> The number of the Children of Israel shall be like the sand of the sea, which cannot be measured or counted....[3]

---

1. Bamidbar 1:1.
2. Bamidbar 1:2.
3. Hoshea 2:1.

The Gemara[4] asks: How is it that they cannot be counted and yet they have a number?

The Gemara answers: When they don't do Hashem's Will, they have a number. When they do His will they cannot be counted.

Rashi seems to contradict the Haftarah. When we have a number it is because we don't fulfill Hashem's Will, how can Rashi say that Hashem counts us because He cherishes us?

To find the answer, let us look at two points from the Ramban:[5]

1) Literally, the words Se'u et rosh ("Take a census") mean "Raise the head." This can mean promotion to greatness, as in "Pharaoh will raise your head and restore you to your post."[6] Or it can mean execution, as in "Pharaoh will raise your head from upon you and hang you."[7]

2) Hashem instructed that every individual be accorded honor as he was being counted. Moshe Rabbenu and Aaron HaKohen visited each one, learned his name, and prayed for him. In addition, he acquired the merit of being recorded as part of the Jewish people.

Accordingly, we may explain the "raising of heads" as follows.

A Jew who has the privilege of a *tzaddik*'s visit is uplifted and inspired. Having received an upward boost, he must climb up the spiritual ladder until he becomes a new person — one so great that he is considered equivalent to many.

Thus Bilaam said, "Who has counted the dust of Yaakov!"[8] That is, they have become so great that it is impossible to count them.

---

4. *Yoma* 82b.
5. On Bamidbar 1:2,3,45.
6. Bereshit 40:13.
7. Bereshit 40:19.
8. Bamidbar 23:10.

So the Haftarah says, "The number of the Children of Israel shall be like the sand of the sea, which cannot be measured or counted." If the Jews were at a relatively low level, like the sand, the counting will prompt him to climb to the level that he "cannot be measured or counted."

If he stays at the same "number" as before the count there is accusation against him: He was given a fantastic opportunity and didn't use it.

This explains *Se'u et rosh,* "Take a census" or "Raise the head." Counting can mean promotion to greatness — but it can also mean execution.

Thus when King David counted the Jewish people, surely he did so with shekels for atonement, as the Torah commands: "When you take a census..., every man shall give Hashem an atonement... so that there will not be a plague...."[9] Yet there was a plague. Why?

Counting the Jewish people is forbidden unless the purpose is to elevate them. And since King David didn't take the census himself they weren't elevated and the count served no purpose.

Now back to Rashi's comment.

"Because they are cherished by Him, He counts them." Why is this comment on the first verse, "Hashem spoke to Moshe in the Sinai desert"? To hint that the desired effect is achieved by Moshe visiting the people to count them.

Rashi continues: "When they fell after the [sin of the golden] calf, He counted them to know how many were left." But we do not find that a census was taken after the sin of the golden calf!

Siftei Hachamim explains: The Torah says, "There fell from the

---

9. Shemot 30:12.

people... about three thousand men."[10] From the number of the fallen, we know the number that were left.

We may add that after this terrible sin and its aftermath, all the people began to mull over what they had done and how low they had fallen, and they were deeply upset. Their thoughts of repentance that elevated them were considered like a census.

Rashi continues: "And when He came to rest His presence on them, He counted them." When the *Shechinah* came to rest upon the Jewish people, it was a time of wonderful joy. Moshe advanced them further by visiting them and taking the census described in our Parashah.

"Because they are cherished by Him, He counts them *at all times*." Whenever a person is inspired and thoughts of repentance enter his heart, it is as if Hashem is counting him. Sometimes Hashem "counts him" through tragedy and grief; other times, though joy. Either way, his heart opens, and he must grab the opportunity to climb higher.

Thus we begin the Humash of Counting. This Humash relates several times that the Jewish people sinned (Korah, the Spies, the Complainers, the daughters of Moav), with tragic aftermaths. But let's remember that "When they fell after the [sin of the golden] calf, He counted them." Every tragedy, then or today, is a "counting" — an opportunity to wake up, make a reckoning, and advance in the service of Hashem, because we are cherished by Him.

OUR INNER DESIRE

Take a census of the entire assembly of the Children of Israel according to their families....[11]

---

10. Shemot 32:25.
11. Bamidbar 1:1–2.

The *Yalkut Shimoni*[12] says that when Israel received the Torah, the nations of the world were jealous. Why should the Jewish people be closer to Hashem than they are?

Hashem closed the nations' mouths by telling them, "Bring me the records of your genealogy" — as it is written, "Bring to Hashem families of nations"[13] — just as My children are bringing — as it is written, "They established their genealogy by their families."[14]

That is why, continues *Yalkut Shimoni*, Hashem counted Israel here. Humash Vayikra ends: "These are the mitzvot that Hashem commanded Moshe to the Children of Israel on Mount Sinai,"[15] and Bamidbar begins with the command to count them "according to their families." Why? Because they received the Torah on Mount Sinai only in the merit of their genealogy.

Now this is puzzling. For the Gemara[16] relates that Hashem offered the Torah to the nations of the world. They asked, "What is written in it?" When they heard, they said, "It doesn't suit us." Then Hashem offered it to the Jews, who accepted it with no questions asked, saying, *Naaseh venishma*.[17] If so, why did the nations complain?

The Gemara says that in the future, when Hashem will reward those who keep the Torah, the nations will complain. "You forced the Jews to accept the Torah, by turning the mountain upside down over their heads like a barrel. Why didn't you do the same to us?"

The *Yalkut Shimoni* answers their argument.

12. 684.
13. Tehilim 96:7.
14. Bamidbar 1:18.
15. Vayikra 27:34.
16. *Avodah Zarah* 2b.
17. "We will do and [then] we will hear" (Shemot 24:7).

The Forefathers, who served Hashem with *mesirut nefesh*,[18] implanted the desire to serve Him in their offspring. Thanks to his genealogy, deep inside every Jew lies a true desire to do Hashem's Will.

The proof comes from the Halachah about a husband who is required to divorce his wife but refuses. The Rambam[19] says that he is to be lashed until he agrees — and this is not considered coercion! Why? Because his true desire is to obey Hashem; his *yetzer*[20] forced him not to. Lashing him weakens the grip of the *yetzer* so that he can fulfill his true desire.

This explains why Hashem forced only the Jews to accept the Torah. After Hashem forced them, they kept the Torah willingly. Had Hashem forced the nations, they would have kept it against their will. Their mitzvah performance would have been external.

The Gemara continues: In days to come, the nations will ask Hashem to give them a mitzvah. He will oblige by giving them an easy one — sukkah. Each will go and build a sukkah on his roof. Then Hashem will bring insufferable heat. Each will immediately kick his sukkah and leave it.

But a Jew who is in distress in the sukkah also leaves, for that is the Halachah!

The difference is that the Jew is upset that he can't fulfill the mitzvah, which he longs to do. The gentile kicks the sukkah, proving that his mitzvah acceptance is external.

The reading of Parashat Bamidbar usually falls before Shavuot. This is no accident. This Parashah speaks of our genealogy, through which we have an inner desire to serve Hashem. This is what makes us alone worthy of receiving the Torah.

---

18. Self-sacrificing devotion.
19. *Hilchot Gerushin* 2:20.
20. Evil inclination.

BANNERS AND CAMPS

The Children of Israel shall encamp, each man at his banner according to the insignias of their fathers' house, at a distance surrounding the Tent of Meeting shall they camp.[21]

The Torah was divided into Parshiot to be read on Shabbat, and the reading was organized, says the Rambam,[22] so that Parashat Bamidbar is to be read before Shavuot.

Why? What does Bamidbar have to do with the giving of the Torah?

To answer, let's first examine the contents of the Parashah.

Bamidbar describes the encampment of the Jewish people as they journeyed through the desert in a square formation. Every group of three Shevatim had its own flag with its own color, and its own place. In the center of them all stood the Mishkan.

Parashat Bamidbar describes the census before describing the encampment. The Zohar says that the Jewish people were counted before Hashem gave them the Torah at Mount Sinai and before He rested His *Shechinah* on them in the Mishkan. This is hinted in the opening verses: "Hashem spoke to Moshe in the Sinai desert in the Tent of Meeting, saying: Take a census...." The Tur says that the census is read before Shavuot.

How are the encampment and the census connected to the giving of the Torah?

I would answer as follows.

Before the giving of the Torah, the Jewish people camped before the mountain "as one man with one heart." Unity was a precondition for receiving the Torah. But what is the Torah ideal of unity?

---

21. Bamidbar 2:2.
22. *Hilchot Tefillah* 13:2.

First, this is what it is not. It is not a giant fish swallowing little fishes so that they will all become one. It is not Communist Russia swallowing its smaller neighbors to become one United Soviet Socialist Republic.

It is not the unity of the generation of the dispersion, whose people united to build a great tower. When a brick fell, they mourned for it, but when a worker fell, they jeered at him. This is the unity of the wicked, where the individual is merely a cog in a wheel.

In the Torah ideal of unity, each individual counts. He is important even though he is different from the next one — moreover, precisely because he is different!

Hashem created people whose opinions are as different as their faces. Each person comes into the world with a unique mission, which no one before him or after him can carry out.

Because he is different, I must love him. For only through every individual fulfilling his mission can the mosaic of the world become complete and reach perfection.

When Moshe counted the Jewish people, he took half a shekel from each for communal sacrifices. This teaches that each of us is only a half, and he needs the other half in order to be completed.

We are called Bet Yisrael, "the House of Israel." It takes many different items to collectively form a house. And it takes many different congregations, each with its own unique banner, to collectively form the Jewish nation.

At the end of his life, Yaakov Avinu saw his sons, each so different from the other, and worried. How could a nation be built from twelve Shevatim who are so different from one another?

They declared, "*Shema,* Hear, O Israel, Hashem is our God, Hashem is One." We are different from one another because each has a different function to fulfill, and the House of Israel can be built only from these collective functions. Although we are all different, we are united in serving Hashem.

Our Sages taught that in the future, Hashem will make a circle for the righteous, and all will point to the center and say, "This is Hashem, Whom we have awaited."[23] Note that the righteous do not form a straight line. Each one is in a different place, but all point to the center.

How tragic it is that instead of loving others because they are different from us, we hate them!

When Yosef was reunited with his brothers, "he wept in a loud voice."[24] Says the Midrash:[25] Just as Yosef appeased his brothers with weeping, so Hashem will redeem Israel with weeping, as it is written, "With weeping they will come, and through supplications I will bring them."[26]

Why will our long-awaited redemption be with weeping, and what does it have to do with Yosef?

The answer ought to shake us up.

When the brothers were reunited with Yosef, they regretted having hated him and sold him. They wept and said, "Why didn't we overcome the dissension between us? We could have saved ourselves years of suffering!"

In the future, we will regret our *sinat hinam*,[27] which has kept us in exile. We will weep and say, "Why didn't we overcome the dissension among us? We could have saved ourselves two thousand years of suffering!"

23. Yeshayahu 25:9.
24. Bereshit 45:2.
25. *Bereshit Rabbah*, Vayigash 93:13.
26. Yirmiyahu 31:8.
27. Groundless hatred.

PARASHAT

Nasso

THE NAZIR

A man or woman who shall separate himself by taking a Nazirite vow of abstinence [from wine] for the sake of Hashem ....[1]

Says Rashi: Why does the law of the Nazir follow immediately after the laws of the Sotah[2]? To tell you that whoever sees the Sotah in her ruin should become a Nazir and separate himself from wine, which leads to immorality.

This implies that whoever only hears about a Sotah need not become a Nazir. I would have thought it would be the other way around. Shouldn't seeing the ruinous results of wine shake a person so that he does not need to become a Nazir?

But it doesn't work that way, for a person sees through the eyes that he has trained.

The story is told of a father who drank too much, embarrassing the family with his behavior. One day, when he was sober, his son took him to see a drunkard who was sprawled on the ground, surrounded by jeering children. Surely such a sight would deter the father from ever touching a bottle again!

---

1. Bamidbar 6:2.
2. Wayward woman.

To the son's chagrin, the father bent down to the drunkard and asked him, "What did you drink to reach such a joyous state?"

At the other end of the spectrum is Rabbi Akiva, who had sanctified his eyes until they were very holy. When Rabbi Akiva saw a woman who was not dressed modestly, he felt so disgusted and nauseated that he spat.[3]

Every person must sanctify his eyes. About *tzitzit*, the Torah says, "You shall see it, and you shall remember all the mitzvot of Hashem and you shall do them."[4] Our eyes must be so holy that if we just look at *tzitzit*, we will be reminded of the heavens, all the way up to Hashem's throne.

In short, the Torah advises us to take action to strengthen ourselves against unwanted influences. It is not enough to say, "Heaven help us."

It is told that the Mashgiah of Slobodka once walked by a store in which a kosher salami was hanging. He felt a desire for it — and immediately vowed not to eat salami for twenty-five years.

When the twenty-five years were over, he said, "Another twenty-five years will do no harm, for the verse says, 'Lust broken pleases the soul.'[5] Rabbenu Yonah explains how: By improving a person's *midot*."

Hovot HaLevavot[6] says: A person should take himself to task for letting the love of this world enter his heart and overpower his love for the world to come. He should set things right and make his love of the world-to-come predominate.

The man who sees the Sotah in her ruin now knows where the lust for wine and immorality lead. He takes action to rein himself

---

3. *Nedarim* 50b.
4. Bamidbar 15:37.
5. Mishlei 13:19.
6. Shaar Heshbon HaNefesh 25.

in and overcome the pull to the love of this world by becoming a Nazir.

In our verse, we find the unusual word יפליא, "separate himself." Tracing the root to פלא, "a wonder," the Ibn Ezra explains that separating himself from wine is a wondrous thing, for most people are drawn after their lusts.

The Torah calls the Nazir holy: "All the days of his abstinence, he is holy to Hashem."[7]

But this contradicts a Gemara,[8] which discusses the verse "He shall atone for him for having sinned regarding the person."[9]

The Gemara asks: Against which person has the Nazir sinned?

It answers: Against himself, because he distressed himself by abstaining from wine. If abstaining from wine is called sinning, surely one who abstains from all food and drink by fasting is called a sinner! From here we learn that whoever fasts is called a sinner.

How can he be a sinner and holy at the same time?

We may answer in light of an episode from the Gemara.[10]

A Nazir once told Shimon HaTzaddik the reason for his vow:

"I was a shepherd for my father in my town. Once I went to draw water from a well and saw the reflection of my beautiful hair in the water. My evil inclination rushed upon me and sought to drive me from the world. I said to it, 'Wretch! Why do you boast in a world that is not yours, with one who is destined to become worms and dust? I swear that I will shave you off for the sake of heaven [by becoming a Nazir; for after the period of the vow ends, a Nazir must shave his head].'"

This righteous Nazir taught us that a person should speak to

---

7. Bamidbar 6:8.
8. *Nedarim* 10a.
9. Bamidbar 6:11.
10. *Nedarim* 9b.

his body and his evil inclination as if he were speaking to someone else. In this way, he rules over his body.

The Hafetz Hayyim *zt"l* did just that. He would say, "Yisrael Meir, what will you answer on the day of judgment?"

When Hillel HaZaken went to eat, he would say, "I am going to do an act of kindness for a guest who is with me." Thus he fulfilled the mitzvah of *hachnasat orhim*[11] every day.[12]

But while we must work on our *midot* and rein in our physical desires, we must also take good care of our body.

The Hovot HaLevavot says that both the soul and the body require care and thought. The soul is strengthened and helped by providing it with Mussar, Torah, and fine *midot;* the body, by providing it with suitable food, bathing it, and meeting its needs.

The body is our vehicle for serving Hashem. Thus the Torah says, "You shall be very careful with your lives."[13] So we eat a good meal — not to indulge our lust but to be strong and healthy to do mitzvot.

What if a person needs to rein in his desires by not drinking wine for at least thirty days (or to fast in order to atone for his sins)?

The Torah allows him to become a Nazir (or to fast) — but he must repent for having deprived his body.

BIRKAT KOHANIM

Speak to Aaron and his sons, saying: Thus shall you bless the Children of Israel. Say to them: "May Hashem bless you and protect you...."

---

11. Extending hospitality.
12. *Vayikra Rabbah* 3:3.
13. Devarim 4:15.

They shall place My Name upon the Children of Israel, and I will bless them.[14]

Even after the Temple was destroyed, one part of the Temple service has remained with us — the priestly blessings.

Says *Sefer Haredim*:[15] It is a mitzvah for the Kohanim to bless the people, as it is written, "Thus shall you bless the Children of Israel."

And what about the people who receive the blessing?

Sefer Haredim continues: The people who stand silently facing the Kohanim — with the intention of receiving the blessing as Hashem said — are also fulfilling a mitzvah.

And the Aruch HaShulhan says: Whoever is not interested in receiving the blessing deserves to be punished for spurning Hashem's blessing.

The Keli Yakar comments that from the words, "Say to them," our Sages learn that the Hazan dictates the blessing to the Kohanim word for word. Thus the Hazan is an agent who draws down blessing from On High and "pours" it onto the Kohanim, making them "full vessels" who in turn "pour" blessing onto the Children of Israel.

Our passage continues: "They shall place My Name upon the Children of Israel, and I will bless them." From here the Gemara[16] learns that Hashem desires the priestly blessing.

How so?

Picture a billionaire telling his impoverished nephew, "I'll give you the money you need; just fill out this form." Hashem is telling us, as it were, "I will bless you; just let the Kohanim say these words."

---

14. Bamidbar 6:23–27.
15. Cited by *Beiur Halachah, Shulhan Aruch, Orah Hayyim* 128; see also *Pit'hei Teshuvah*.
16. *Sotah* 38b.

The Gemara[17] relates that the Kohen Gadol, Rabbi Yishmael ben Elisha, related: "I once entered the Holy of Holies on Yom Kippur to offer incense... and Hashem said to me, 'Yishmael My son, bless Me.'

"I said to Him, 'May it be Your Will... that You treat Your children with...mercy....'"[18]

For Hashem desires that we ask Him to bestow good on the Jewish people.

Similarly, the *Mesilat Yesharim*[19] says: Hashem is pleased when His children pray for Mashiah and the final redemption. He wants them to "seek Tzion." From the verse "She is Tzion — no one seeks her,"[20] our Sages learn that seeking is necessary. Even if the request is not fulfilled because the time is not yet ripe (or for any other reason), Hashem is happy that we have done our part.

It follows that when we send the Kohanim to ask Hashem to bless us we are doing Hashem's Will. In fact, both we and the Kohanim fulfill a *mitzvat aseh,* as the Sefer Haredim said.

Our passage ends: "And I will bless them." Whom will Hashem bless?

The Gemara[21] cites two opinions.

Rabbi Yishmael ben Elisha says that Hashem will bless the Kohanim.

Rabbi Akiva says that He will agree with the Kohanim's request and bless the Jewish people. As for the Kohanim themselves, when they bless they are automatically blessed, for Hashem told Avraham, "I will bless those who bless you."[22]

17. *Berachot* 7a.
18. *Berachot* 7a.
19. Chapter 19.
20. Yirmiyahu 30:17.
21. *Hulin* 49a.
22. Bereshit 12:3.

In summary, Hashem wants us to ask Him to bless us (as we do in the priestly blessings) and to redeem us (as we do in the Amidah). David HaMelech said, "I love that Hashem hears my voice, my supplications."[23] The verse does not say "I love that Hashem grants my supplications," but that He hears them. Ours is to supplicate. At the right time, blessing and redemption will come.

TWELVE IDENTICAL OFFERINGS

...on the first day... Nahshon ben Amindav, of the Tribe of Yehudah. His offering: one silver bowl, its weight 130....[24]

On the second day, Netanel ben Tzuar, the Nassi of Issachar... his offering: one silver bowl, its weight 130...[25]

On the twelfth day, the Nassi of the children of Naphtali, Ahira ben Enan. His offering: one silver bowl, its weight 130....[26]

As part of the dedication of the Mishkan, the heads of the Tribes brought twelve identical offerings. The Torah could have saved 55 verses by saying, "Each Nassi brought his offering: one silver bowl, its weight 130...." Why does the Torah record their offerings twelve times?

The Hafetz Hayyim answered that Netanel ben Tzuar, who brought his offering on the second day, advised them all to bring identical offerings to prevent jealousy. Hashem was so pleased that he told them, "You took action to preserve brotherhood and friendship, so I will honor each of you."

The Midrash[27] answers that although physically the offerings

---

23. Tehilim 116:1.
24. Bamidbar 7:12–17.
25. Bamidbar 7:18–23.
26. Bamidbar 7Behaalotecha:78–83.
27. *Bamidbar Rabbah* 14.

were the same, in reality they were totally different. For each Nassi had unique lofty *kavanot*[28] pertaining specifically to his Tribe. Here we see a fundamental principle: that the *kavanah* changes the whole deed.

I heard a third answer from Rabbi Dan Segal *shlita* in the name of Rabbi Shmuel Rozovsky *zt"l.*

Usually if there is only one *tzaddik* in a city, he is honored greatly, but if there are many *tzaddikim*, each is honored less. Here, even though there were twelve *tzaddikim*, the Torah honored each fully, as if he were the only one.

So by repeating the same offering twelve times, the Torah teaches us the correct perspective. Hashem wants us to love one another and avoid jealousy; *kavanah* is extremely important; and we must honor each *tzaddik* greatly, as if there are no other *tzaddikim*.

---

28. Intents.

PARASHAT

Behaalotecha

AARON'S ROLE

Hashem spoke to Moshe, saying, "Speak to Aaron and say to him: When you kindle the lamps, toward the face of the Menorah shall the seven lamps cast light."

Aaron did so; toward the face of the Menorah he kindled its lamps, as Hashem had commanded Moshe.

This is the workmanship of the Menorah: *mikshah* — a single piece of beaten gold — from its base to its flower....[1]

The Ohr HaHayyim asks: Why do we need both "speak to Aaron" and "say to him"?

Moreover, why does the Torah need to tell us that Aaron obeyed? Rashi answers: "To praise Aaron for not changing." What didn't Aaron change? And why does the Torah say so only in connection with tilting the wicks toward the center?

Finally, why does the Torah speak here of the Menorah being *mikshah*, a single piece of beaten gold? The subject at hand is lighting the Menorah, not making it. The workmanship is discussed in Parashat Terumah!

There is one answer to all these questions.

---

1. Bamidbar 8:1–4.

Our Sages say: When Aaron saw that the Nessi'im brought offerings for the dedication of the Mishkan, he was distraught, for he and his Tribe had not been part of the dedication. Hashem said to him, "Yours is greater than theirs, for you prepare the lamps and kindle them."

In what way is Aaron's mitzvah of preparing and kindling the lamps greater than the offerings of the Nessi'im?

To find out, let us look into the offerings of the Nessi'im.

The Midrash[2] says: Even though all twelve Nessi'im brought identical offerings, they had different lofty *kavanot* when they brought them. For instance, the Davidic dynasty would issue from the Tribe of Yehudah. So the *kavanot* of its Nassi were about kingship, Shelomo HaMelech, and Mashiah.

Although the twelve offerings were all identical externally, in reality they were all different because the roles of the Tribes were all different.

At the same time, they were expected to work together to serve Hashem.

The Hafetz Hayyim compared the Jewish nation to an army. Each army unit has its own role and may not switch to a different one. At the same time, each unit must treat all the other units with respect and affection, and cooperate with them to win the war.

Similarly, the Jewish nation consists of many different groups. Each group has its own role and may not switch to a different one. At the same time, each group must treat all the other groups with respect and affection, and cooperate with them to serve Hashem.

Aaron, too, had his own role and was not to switch to another one. This explains why Hashem told Moshe both "speak (*daber*) to Aaron" and "say (*ve'amarta*) to him." *Daber* is tough; *ve'amarta*

---

2. *Bamidbar Rabbah* 13:14.

is gentle. *Ve'amarta* was to inform Aaron of his role. *Daber* was to warn him not to switch.

Rashi says: "To praise Aaron for not changing" — for not changing his role.

What was the role of Aaron and his descendants?

To tilt all the wicks toward the center of the Menorah, and to unite all the different groups and turn them toward Hashem — which is the inner aspect of tilting the wicks.

The Menorah itself, too, has an external aspect and an inner one. Externally, it looks as if it has many different parts: base, shaft, cups, knob, and flowers. But in reality, it is all *mikshah* — one piece of beaten gold.

Aaron's role is extremely important. For it is well and good for each Nassi to have different *kavanot* in accordance with his Tribe's role. But there is a danger that each will pull away from the rest, claiming, "My way is the right one; everyone else's is wrong." There must be someone who unites them — who "loves peace and pursues peace"[3] and goes and tells each one the other's good points — so that all will work together to sanctify Hashem's Name.

AARON IS COMFORTED

Hashem spoke to Moshe, saying, "Speak to Aaron and say to him: When you kindle [*behaalotecha*, literally: when you elevate] the lamps, toward the face of the Menorah shall the seven lamps cast light."[4]

Our Sages say: When Aaron saw that the Nessi'im brought offerings for the dedication of the Mishkan, he was distraught, for

---

3. *Avot* 1:12.
4. Bamidbar 8:1.

he and his Tribe had not been part of the dedication. Hashem said to him, "Yours is greater than theirs, for you prepare the lamps and kindle them."

How was this a comfort to Aaron?

To answer this question, let's examine the idea of giving Hashem light.

The Gemara[5] notes that Hashem told Moshe, "They shall take *for you* pure olive oil"[6] — the oil should be for you not for Me. Hashem said: There shall be a Menorah in the Mishkan, but I do not need light. And there shall be a Table, but I do not need bread.

Who would think otherwise? Surely the Creator of the sun does not need our light! And the Creator of wheat does not need our bread!

The Midrash[7] quotes Hashem as saying, "My children, do for Me as I have done for you. I fed you meat in the desert — you offer the daily *Tamid* sacrifice. I rained down manna — you put *lehem hapanim* on the Table. I went before You in a pillar of fire — you kindle the Menorah."

What Hashem was saying was don't think I need your service of kindling the lights in order to give My children the pillar of fire, or I need your service of presenting the bread in order to give them manna. In fact, I gave these things to My children in the desert even before they built the Mishkan.

If Hashem did not need the light of the Menorah in order to give His children a pillar of fire, why *did* he command that the Menorah be kindled?

The Midrash[8] gives two answers. One is "to elevate you in the

---

5. *Menahot* 86b.
6. Shemot 27:20.
7. *Tanhuma, Tetzaveh* 1.
8. *Tanhuma, Behaalotecha* 2,4.

eyes of the nations. They will say, 'See how Israel gives light to He Who lights up the world.'" The other is "to bring you merit. So be careful to do it for the sake of My Name, and I will shine brilliant light for you in times to come."

This is how Hashem comforted Aaron. Each Nassi, with his offering, had acquired merit only for his own Tribe.[9] But by kindling the Menorah, Aaron would do two great things for the entire Jewish people: elevate them in the eyes of the nations and bring them brilliant light in the world to come.

---

9. See *Bamidbar Rabbah*, Nasso.

PARASHAT

Shelah

LOOK FOR THE GOOD

"Send forth for yourself men, and let them spy out the Land of Canaan that I am giving to the Children of Israel...."[1]

What did the Spies do wrong in delivering a negative report about the Holy Land? The Ramban[2] says that they spoke the truth. Moshe Rabbenu had sent them to spy out the Land — surely he did not want them to falsify their report!

Moshe commanded them:[3] "See the Land — how is it? And the people that dwells in it — is it strong or weak? Is it few of numerous? And how is the Land in which it dwells — is it good or bad?"

"Strong or weak?" — The Spies saw giants. The Midrash[4] relates that the giant Talmai shouted at the Spies, who fell fainting as a result. Other men came, resuscitated the Spies, and revived them. So of course the Spies reported that the people of the Land were mighty.

"Few or numerous?" — Rashi explains: Does the Land increase

---

1. Bamidbar 13:2.
2. Bereshit 2:9.
3. Bamidbar 13:18–19.
4. *Yalkut Shimoni.*

97

population or decrease it? That is, are there plagues that diminish the population? Everywhere the Spies went, they saw funerals. True, Hashem arranged this phenomenon so that the inhabitants would not notice the Spies. But no heavenly voice explained this to the Spies. So of course they reported that it is "a land that devours its inhabitants."[5]

"Good or bad?" — How could Moshe ask such a question? Why didn't he tell them to see how good the Land is?

Let's begin our quest for the answer with Rabbenu Yonah,[6] who discusses the verse "Fools suggest guilt, but there is favor among the straight."[7] Fools look for the faults and guilt in people and speak ill of them, like flies who are attracted to garbage. Those who are straight look for good points and speak about them.

This explains an interesting phenomenon. Several people are in the same place at the same time. The place might be a private home, a public institution, or a shul. Some of these people will praise the place or the people in charge of it; the others will criticize it. How is this possible?

Rabbenu Yonah explains that the reaction depends on the person's character. A fool has a flaw in himself. He is like a fly, who lives off the filth. He sees only guilt, and that is what he speaks about.

In the early days of the Jewish people, a person who spoke *lashon hara* would be afflicted with *tzaraat*. He would live in isolation, without even the company of another *metzora*.[8] But since Hashem's punishments are measure for measure, why was he given *tzaraat* rather than pain in his mouth? And why was he isolated?

---

5. Bamidbar 13:32.
6. Shaarei Teshuvah 3:217.
7. Mishlei 14:9.
8. Person afflicted with *tzaraat*.

Because while sitting alone, he will think about why his only visitors are flies. He will notice that they alight on the afflicted parts of his skin, and that although he shoos them away, they keep coming back. Hopefully he will begin to realize that he, too, has the personality of a fly, and then he will repent and fix his *midot*.

A fool focuses not only on the bad in other people, but also on the bad in his own life. He is dissatisfied, bitter, and full of complaints against Hashem.

In contrast, "there is favor among the straight." A person whose thinking is straight knows that the other fellow has many good points, which he looks for and speaks about. Instead of finding fault and criticizing, he finds the good and praises. He also thinks a lot about the wonderful things in his own life, as the Hovot Ha-Levavot[9] tells us to do. He lives in a state of favor — he is happy in life.

The Hafetz Hayyim once asked a visitor, "How are you?"

"On the spiritual side, all is well," replied the visitor. "I pray with a minyan and keep fixed times for Torah study; Shabbat and Yom Tov are in order. But on the material realm, things are tough."

The Hafetz Hayyim told him, "What you are saying is that you fulfill your obligations to Hashem, but He does not fulfill His obligations to you."

The visitor was astounded by the truth in these words.

Rabbenu Yonah continues: Two men once passed an animal's carcass. One said, "What a foul odor!" The other, who was wise, said, "What beautiful teeth!"

There is certainly no prohibition against speaking ill of a dead animal. What, then, was the wise man's point?

That if you do not want to suffer from the foul odor, focus on

---

9. *Shaar Heshbon HaNefesh,* ch. 1.

how beautiful the teeth are. In life, whoever sticks his nose into foul smells will suffer from it. If you want to be happy, see only the good.

Now back to the Spies.

Moshe said, "Is it good or bad?" He did not mean: Check whether the Land is good. Of course it is very, very good! He meant: Check your way of looking. What do *you* see in the Land of Israel? Are you happy with Hashem's gift? If not, then the time is not ripe for you to enter the Land.

The Spies should have understood that everything Hashem did was for their own good. When they saw the giants, they should have interpreted it in a positive way and said, "This is a very healthy land; it produces mighty people." When they saw funerals, they should have realized that He was distracting the populace, even without a heavenly voice telling them.

In this way, they would have rejoiced over everything they saw in the Land.

The Gemara[10] relates that a peddler announced that he was selling an elixir of life. When everyone came, the peddler took out a volume of Tehilim and read the passage:[11]

> Who is the man who desires life, who loves days, to see good.
> Guard your tongue from evil....

Rabbi Yanai was deeply impressed by this peddler. But why? The peddler had merely quoted a passage that the Sage already knew!

We may answer that Rabbi Yannai had thought the passage was speaking of life in the world to come. Along came a peddler, who sold wares that make life in this world more comfortable and

---

10. *Avodah Zarah* 19b.
11. Tehilim 34:13–14.

also read this passage, as if to say: This passage shows how to live a comfortable, pleasant life in this world. The peddler read the verse this way:

> Who is the man who desires life, who loves days? [The solution is] to see good.

See the good. Notice the beautiful teeth of a dead animal rather than its foul odor. When you live this way, you will always be happy in life.

However according to the classic interpretation the two verses refer to the world to come. If so, the question and answer don't match! The world to come consists of Gan Eden — the reward for mitzvot, and Gehinnom — the punishment for sins. If the question is who wants life in Gan Eden, the answer should be "Do mitzvot." And if the answer is "Guard your tongue from evil" — that is, don't sin — the question should be who doesn't want Gehinnom.

We may explain based on the Hovot HaLevavot's[12] teaching that when a person speaks *lashon hara*, all his mitzvot are transferred to his victim. Accordingly, our passage asks: Who wants to receive Gan Eden for his mitzvot? And the answer is: Don't speak *lashon hara*, for if you do, your mitzvot will go to your victim.

CALEV AND YEHOSHUA

> These are their names... For the Tribe of Yehudah, Calev ben Yephuneh.... For the Tribe of Ephraim, Hoshea bin Nun.[13]

What helped Calev and Yehoshua stand firm and not be swept by along by the overwhelming majority?

---

12. *Shaar HaKeniah*, ch. 7.
13. Bamidbar 13:4–8.

Yehoshua drank in his teacher's words thirstily as the verse says, "His [Moshe's] attendant Yehoshua bin Nun, a youth, would not move from within the tent."[14] Moshe was like the sun; Yehoshua, like the moon, which receives its light from the sun. Thus since Moshe had called Eretz Yisrael "a land of milk and honey,"[15] Yehoshua had no doubts.

In addition, Moshe prayed that Yehoshua be saved from the persuasion of the ten Spies. He did not pray for the ten Spies, because they needed to do serious work to fix themselves.

As for Calev, he was from the Tribe of Yehudah. When Yehudah (יהודה) was born, his mother, Leah Imenu, said, "This time I shall thank (אודה) Hashem,"[16] and she named him accordingly. The Gemara[17] says: From the day Hashem created His world, there was no one who thanked Hashem until Leah came and thanked him.

Leah brought up Yehudah to understand that the essence of a Jew — *Yehudi,* "one who thanks" — is to recognize his Creator and the goodness that He bestows on him. From the moment he opens his eyes in the morning until he closes them at night, a Jew should be thanking and praising Hashem.

Yehudah's descendant David HaMelech instituted saying a hundred blessings a day with which to recognize His kindnesses and thank Him for them. It begins with the morning blessings. In "Who gives sight to the blind," we thank Him that we can see; in "Who firms a man's steps," we thank Him that we can walk. And so on.

Since such was Calev's upbringing, naturally his eyes saw only the good in the Land of Israel. And when he went to pray in Hevron, he surely prayed about this at Leah's grave.

---

14. Shemot 33:11.
15. Shemot 13:5.
16. Bereshit 29:35.
17. *Berachot* 7b.

There are two messages here: to follow in the way of Yehoshua by listening to the *gedol hador*; and to follow in the way of Caleb, by reciting a hundred blessings a day with *kavanah*.

THE "ADVICE" OF THE SPIES

"They returned from spying out the Land at the end of forty days. They went and they came to Moshe...."[18]

Did the Spies start out being righteous or wicked?

On our verse, Rashi comments: What is meant by "They went"? To compare their going to their coming. Just as they came with evil counsel, so they went with evil counsel.

If so, they were not righteous to begin with.

But when Moshe sent them, the Torah says "All of them were men,"[19] from which Rashi learns: "At that time, they were righteous"!

We can solve the contradiction based on the following *Yalkut Shimoni*,[20] which cites Moshe's account of how the episode began (in Humash Devarim[21]):

All of you approached me and said, "Let us send men ahead of us, and let them spy out (ויחפרו) the Land..."
The matter was good in my eyes....

The unusual word used here for "spy out" literally means "dig."

Based on this, the *Yalkut* says: When Moshe asked the people why they wanted to send Spies, they replied, "Hashem promised that when we enter the Land, He will give us 'houses filled with

---

18. Bamidbar 13:25–26.
19. Bamidbar 13:3.
20. *Shelah* 13.
21. Devarim 1:22–23.

every good thing that you did not fill.'[22] But the Canaanites, having heard that we are coming, are burying their valuables. If we find nothing, *Hashem's word will not be fulfilled.* Let us send Spies to see where they are digging."

We may add that "The matter was good in my eyes" because it seemed that their intention was for the sake of heaven.

Let us continue the line of thought presented in the *Yalkut* and expand on it, as we examine how the episode developed.

Moshe Rabbenu took twelve men and instructed them:[23] "See the Land — how is it? And the people who dwell in it — are they strong or weak? Are they few or numerous? And how is the Land in which they dwell — is it good or bad?"

The Spies interpreted Moshe's instructions to mean: If conditions are favorable for us, we will enter the Land now. If not, we will wait.

They returned and said, "We have seen some things that will prevent the Jewish people from appreciating the Land properly. The Land's inhabitants are mighty, making waging war in a natural way difficult. When they got to Hevron, the giant Talmai gave a shout, and it took artificial resuscitation to revive us; if Jews want to go to Hevron, will they have to keep resuscitation kits with them at all times? "Amalek, with its terrible sorcery, lives there. And there is pestilence in the Land now." When a person does not appreciate what Hashem gives him, Hashem takes it away. If the Jewish people do not appreciate the Land, and He takes it away, *Hashem's word will not be fulfilled.*"

So the Spies gave Moshe Rabbenu advice: Instead of entering the Land immediately, let's wait a few years and then send Spies again. By then the pestilence will probably be gone....

---

22. Devarim 6:10–11.
23. Bamidbar 13:18–19.

But the Spies had misinterpreted Moshe's instructions to check the Land. Moshe knew that "the Land is very, very good,"[24] as Yehoshua and Calev reported; he was not asking them to check whether it was or wasn't. Rather, Moshe meant: The Land of Israel is full of challenges and is acquired through suffering. If you see that the Land is above our present level, we will have to elevate ourselves spiritually and prepare prayers and *kavanot* with which to enter.[25] Regarding the giants and the sorcerers, for instance, we must have the *kavanah* that they are nothing, and *en od milvado,* "There is none beside Him."[26]

The Jewish people had experience fighting the forces of impurity in the battle against Amalek. "When Moshe raised his hand, Israel was stronger; and when he lowered his hand, Amalek was stronger."[27] Our Sages[28] said: Do Moshe's hands win the battle or lose the battle?! Rather, when the Jewish people looked upward and subjugated their heart to Hashem, they prevailed. But when they did not, they fell.

And so it would be with the wars in the Land of Israel.

Now we can answer our opening question: Did the Spies start out being righteous or wicked?

When they were chosen, they were righteous. But then Moshe gave them instructions, and they misinterpreted his words. Here the wickedness began — with the thought that they were to return and give Moshe advice as to when to enter the Land.

Moshe prayed for Yehoshua, "May Hashem save you from the *etzah* of the Spies."[29] Literally, *etzah* means "advice."

---

24. Bamidbar 14:7.
25. Intents.
26. Devarim 4:35.
27. Shemot 17:12.
28. Mishnah *Rosh HaShannah* 3:8.
29. Rashi, Bamidbar 13:16.

The sin of the Spies lay in giving Moshe Rabbenu advice.

Why did the Spies misinterpret Moshe's words?

The Zohar[30] says that they sought honor, and they feared that in the Land of Israel they would no longer be leaders.

Not that this was their deliberate, conscious intention. Rather, subconsciously they had this *negiah,* self-interest, which caused them to misinterpret. For a person's *negiot* warp his understanding.

To a person with straight understanding, Moshe's intention was clear. For this whole world — filled as it is with falsehood, lusts, and bad character traits — is one big challenge. And the challenge is even greater in the Holy Land. In the palace of the King, one must behave correctly and maintain a high spiritual level at all times.

TZITZIT

They shall make themselves *tzitzit* on the corners of their garments....

...that you may see it and remember all Hashem's mitzvot and do them, and explore not after your heart and after your eyes....

So that you may remember and do all My mitzvot and be holy to your God.

I am Hashem, your God, Who took you out of the land of Egypt to be a God to you; I am Hashem, your God.[31]

Why does our passage tell us twice that *tzitzit* helps us remember and do the mitzvoth, and twice that "I am Hashem, your God"?

The first "remember-and-do" is the reason behind the mitzvah of *tzitzit.* We put on *tefillin* to subjugate our minds and hearts to Hashem; and we wear *tzitzit* to remind us of the Torah's 613 mitzvot. The numerical value of the Hebrew word (צִיצִית) is 600; add

30. Cited in *Mesilat Yesharim,* end of ch. 11.
31. Bamidbar 15:38–41.

the 8 threads and 5 knots, and the result is 613.[32] Wearing *tzitzit* makes a statement: "I hereby undertake to fulfill all 613 mitzvot." No wonder it is considered like keeping the whole Torah.

The second "remember-and-do," which includes "and be holy," is a result of fulfilling the mitzvah of *tzitzit,* just as "So that your days and the days of your children will be multiplied"[33] is a reward for keeping the mitzvot.

From "and be holy," Sifri learns that *tzitzit* adds holiness to the Jewish people.

This additional holiness protects the wearer of *tzitzit* from immorality. Our Sages[34] said that Shem's descendants merited "the tallit of *tzitzit*" because Shem took a garment and covered the nakedness of his father, Noah.[35] Hashem endowed *tzitzit* with the ability to save the wearer from sins of "nakedness," as the Keli Yakar comments.

The Gemara[36] relates that a man who was particular about *tzitzit* was about to sin, when his *tzitzit* saved him by slapping his face. He noted that "I am Hashem, your God" appears twice in connection with *tzitzit,* to teach: It is I Who punish, and it is I Who reward.

Thus "I am Hashem, your God," concludes the second remember-and-do, which speaks of the reward for the mitzvah of *tzitzit.*

We have seen that wearing *tzitzit* is considered like keeping all 613 mitzvot, and that it imbues us with holiness and protects us from sin. But why is it linked to wearing a four-cornered garment?

The Zohar teaches that the four corners of the garment correspond to the "four corners" of the earth. The idea is that whether we turn East, South, West, or North, we should see Hashem.

---

32. Rashi, Bamidbar 15:39.
33. Devarim 11:21.
34. *Bereshit Rabbah* 36:6; see also Rashi.
35. See Bereshit 9:23.
36. *Menahot* 44a.

The Ohr HaHayyim[37] adds: A sign of servitude must show who the master is. *Tzitzit* is our sign of servitude. We make this sign on a four-corned garment to show that our Master is the Creator and Ruler of the four corners of the earth.

No wonder our Sages taught that we should always wear a four-cornered garment in order to obligate ourselves in the mitzvah of *tzitzit* at all times.

---

37. Bamidbar 15:39.

PARASHAT

Korah

THE "TASTE" OF MITZVOT

Vayikah Korah, Korah took....[1]

The verse says, "Korah took," but doesn't tell us what he took. Rashi says: Korah took himself to one side to split off from the congregation and contest Aaron's right to the priesthood.[2] Thus Korah was the first to dissent and arouse contention against the *gedolei hador.*

How did he do it?

The Midrash[3] tells us about Korah's provocation. He dressed his men in garments that were entirely of *techelet*.[4] They stood before Moshe and asked, "Is a garment that is entirely of *techelet* exempt from *tzitzit* or not?" Moshe replied, "The obligation remains." They laughed at him, saying, "Is it possible that four threads of *techelet* exempt the whole garment, but a whole garment of *techelet* does not exempt itself?

Then Korah asked, "If a house is filled with Torah Scrolls, is it

---

1. Bamidbar 16:1.
2. See Rashi, Onkelos.
3. See *Bamidbar Rabbah* 18:3.
4. Sky-blue wool.

exempt from a mezuzah?" Moshe said, "The obligation remains."
Korah said, "Is it possible that a mezuzah exempts the house, but a
whole Torah does not?"

Korah's provocative questions seem to make no sense. It's like
asking, "Is it possible that a bit of grease on a wagon's wheels makes
them turn smoothly, but a whole barrel of grease sitting in the wagon
does not?"

Evidently we need to take a deeper look at Korah's questions.

Many mitzvot have a *taam* — literally: "taste" — that helps us
understand them. Korah wanted to follow the *taam* of the mitzvah.

The color of *techelet* was worn by kings. It shows that Jews are
"a kingdom of priests."[5] And from the words "It shall be for you for
tzitzit,"[6] the Midrash says: To give splendor to your appearance.

To accomplish this, argued Korah, a garment that is entirely
techelet is surely better.

The *taam* of mezuzah is spelled out by the Rambam:[7] Whenever
a person comes in or goes out, he will encounter Hashem's Name.
He will remember to love Him, will wake up from the nonsense of
this temporary world, and will realize that nothing but knowledge
of Hashem endures. So he will immediately return to straight ways.

To accomplish this, argued Korah, a house filled with Torah
Scrolls is surely better.

No, said Moshe. We must fulfill the mitzvot as Hashem said,
regardless of *taam*.

The Mussar authorities added: Nourishment comes from eating
food, not from tasting a bit of it.

---

5. Shemot 19:6.
6. Bamidbar 15:39.
7. *Hilchot Mezuzah* 6:13.

OF HIS OWN VOLITION

Korah son of Yitzhar son of Kehat son of Levi... and ...the descendants of Reuven.[8]

What were Korah and his company trying to achieve?

Korah, who was of distinguished lineage, wanted to be Kohen Gadol instead of Aaron. That is why Moshe told Korah, "You and Aaron, each man with his fire pan."[9] Some of Korah's men, who were of the Tribe of Reuven — Yaakov's firstborn — wanted to do the Levite service. That is why Moshe said, "In the morning, Hashem will make known the one who is His own"[10] — for the Levite service, says Rashi.[11]

How dared they? In fact, Rashi[12] asks, "And Korah, who was clever" enough to draw people to his side through dining and scoffing, "what did he see to do this foolishness?" It's dangerous to try to oust a Kohen Gadol without any reason!

We might answer as follows. They knew Moshe had done three things of his own volition to which Hashem then agreed. He added one day to the days of preparation for receiving the Torah; he separated from his wife; and he broke the Tablets, as the Gemara[13] states.

Korah and his company added a fourth item to the list. They said, "Moshe chose his brother and his Tribe of his own volition, and then Hashem agreed." Now they demanded that Moshe suggest their candidacy for these positions, and surely Hashem would

8. Bamidbar 16:1.
9. Bamidbar 16:17.
10. Bamidbar 16:5.
11. See also Seforno, Ohr HaHayyim, and Rabbenu Behayyei.
12. Bamidbar 16:7.
13. *Shabbat* 87a.

agree. For, as Rashi[14] explains, Korah saw prophetically that from him would issue Shemuel, who is considered equivalent to Moshe and Aaron. If so, surely Korah himself had tremendous merit!

Korah gathered around him wise men of distinguished lineage, "princes of the congregation, who determined times (*keri'ei mo'ed*)" — who knew how to determine the months and intercalate years — "men of renown."[15] They said to Moshe: Why do you take the leadership for yourselves and count us for nothing?

Thus Rashi says:[16]

> *Rav lachem,* "It is too much for you" — you took too much high position for yourselves.
>
> "For the entire congregation — all of them — are holy" — all of us heard [the first two of the Ten] Commandments from Hashem at Sinai.
>
> "Why do you exalt yourselves over Hashem's congregation?" — if you took kingship for yourself, you should not have chosen the priesthood for your brother.

Moshe told them to take fire-pans and offer incense, as if to say: Okay, I am suggesting that Korah be the Kohen Gadol and that you do the Levite service. If Hashem agrees, you win.

But when they offered the incense, its sanctity caused its fire to burn them, for they were not suitable for this holy service. Similarly, Nadav and Avihu died when they offered incense after drinking wine; and in the Second Temple era many unworthy Kohanim Gedolim died in the Holy of Holies. Sanctity itself burns a person who is not suitable for it.

---

14. Bamidbar 16:7.
15. Bamidbar 16:2.
16. Bamidbar 16:3.

DINING AND SCOFFING

Vayikah Korah, Korah bought....[17]

Resh Lakish[18] renders *Vayikah Korah* as "Korah bought" and says: Korah made a bad purchase for himself.

This purchase must have cost Korah a lot of money. For our Sages[19] applied the verse "Wealth kept by its owner is his misfortune"[20] to him.

What did Korah buy?

I would answer that he "bought" 250 prominent men. How? By wining and dining them.

Our Sages[21] says that he invited the 250 men to a feast, at which he scoffed and incited them against Moshe Rabbenu. And he succeeded, for, as the Gemara[22] observes, one can win people over to his veiwpoint by wining and dining them. We find that when Yehoshaphat king of Yehudah went to Ahav king of Yisrael, "Ahav slaughtered a great many sheep and cattle for him and for the people accompanying him — and incited him to go to war against Ramot Gilad."[23]

Korah, too, incited people by making them a feast. And at this feast, he scoffed by telling an imaginary story:[24]

"A poor widow in my neighborhood had two daughters. All she owned was a small field, which provided their livelihood. When she plowed, Moshe came and said, 'Be careful not to plow with an ox and donkey together.' When she planted, Moshe said, 'Be careful

17. Bamidbar 16:1.
18. *Sanhedrin* 109b.
19. *Pesahim* 119a.
20. Kohelet 5:12.
21. *Sanhedrin* 52a.
22. *Hulin* 4b.
23. Divrei HaYamim 1 18:2.
24. See *Me'am Lo'ez.*

not to plant *kilayim*.'[25] When she harvested, Moshe said, 'Be careful to leave *leket, shichehah,* and *peah*.'[26] When she stored the grain, Moshe said, 'You must give *terumah* and the first and second tithes.' She suffered in silence and did as Moshe commanded.

"Then she said, 'It is not worthwhile to keep a field and have so much trouble.' She sold the field and bought two lambs. When they gave birth, Aaron came and said, 'Give me the firstborns.' She suffered in silence and gave him the firstborns. When she sheared the sheep, Aaron said, 'Give me the first shorn wool.' The widow said, 'Until now I have fallen into a trap; now I will slaughter them.' When she slaughtered them, Aaron came again and said, 'Give me the priest's portion of the meat.' 'If so,' she said, 'I consecrate them as a *herem*.[27]' Said Aaron, 'Now give me everything, for Hashem said: Every *herem* in Israel shall be yours.'[28] He took everything she had, and she and her daughters died of starvation."

All this was obviously imaginary, and the listeners knew it. There were no fields to plow in the desert; and there was no hunger, for manna rained down from heaven. Besides, no financial loss comes from separating species as required by the Torah; and the various gifts and tithes to the poor, the Kohanim, and the Levi'im are a relatively small part of one's profits but they build society. The widow in the story is not to be pitied; she made her own problems, throwing away what she owned out of spite. Yet such are the power of dining and the power of scoffing that Korah was able to incite great people against Moshe with this story.

Scoffing is no joke. *Mesilat Yesharim*[29] explains that scoffing

---

25. Forbidden mixtures.
26. For the poor.
27. Vowed as banned.
28. Bamidbar 18:14.
29. Chapter 5.

resembles a shield smeared with oil. If arrows are shot at a person who is behind an oiled shield, they will slip off and fall to the ground without penetrating his body. Scoffing does the same to any rebukes or stirring of conscience; it throws these all to the ground so that they have no impact.

That is why these great men did not accept Moshe's rebuke, and they did not repent. Partying and scoffing can fell even giants.

PAST AND FUTURE

"For the entire congregation — all of them — are holy, and Hashem is in their midst. Why do you exalt yourselves over Hashem's congregation?"[30]

Rashi[31] says that "Korah took" heads of courts, drawing them with his words. If so, there must have been some convincing logic to his viewpoint. What was it?

The answer lies in Rashi's[32] comment: What did Korah, who was clever, see to do this foolishness? He saw that the prophet Shemuel would issue from him.

Let's examine Shemuel's viewpoint.

In Shemuel's time, the Jewish people requested a king. Shemuel became angry, and told them, "Hashem, your God, is your King!"[33]

But the Torah explicitly commands the Jewish people to appoint a king after entering the Land of Israel! "When you come to the Land..., and you say, 'I shall set a king over myself....' You shall surely set a king over yourself...."[34]

---

30. Bamidbar 16:3.
31. Bamidbar 16:1.
32. Bamidbar 16:7.
33. Shemuel 1 12:12.
34. Devarim 17:14–15.

How could Shemuel object to fulfilling a mitzvah? And why, in giving us this mitzvah, does the Torah insert "and you say, 'I shall set a king over myself....'"?

One question answers the other.

A Jewish king must ensure that the mitzvot are kept, and he may inflict severe punishment (lashes or death) for this purpose. Fear of the king forces everyone to toe the line.

But this is far from ideal, as Shemuel explained. It is much better to keep mitzvot out of love for Hashem than out of fear of a human king. Nevertheless, if "you say, 'I shall set a king over myself'" — for you see that the situation has deteriorated to the point where a king is necessary — then a king must indeed be appointed.

Shemuel's ancestor Korah also said: It is much better to keep mitzvot out of love for Hashem than out of fear of a human ruler.

Korah added: When Hashem gave us the Torah, He said, "You shall be for Me a kingdom of priests and a holy nation."[35] Each Jew is to be a king or queen, and the body of mitzvot is the royal protocol. If any Jew gives up the crown, it is his own loss. He should not be forced to keep mitzvot.

Thus Korah said to Moshe and Aaron, "The entire congregation — all of them — are holy. Why do you exalt yourselves over Hashem's congregation?" That is, why do you talk down to them and force them, with stern rebuke, to serve Hashem?

And to the people, Korah said: Give me the leadership, and I will do differently. I will use nothing stronger than gentle persuasion.

(How do we know that Korah wanted to take over the leadership? The Torah only indicates that Korah wanted Aaron's position.[36]

---

35. Shemot 19:6.
36. See also Rashi, Bamidbar 16:5,6.

However, the Gemara[37] indicates that he wanted Moshe's position, too — On ben Pelet was told by his wife not to follow Korah, for "If Moshe is the teacher, you are a disciple, and if Korah is the teacher, you will still be a disciple.")

Korah campaigned against forceful leadership with his imaginary story about the poor widow (see "Dining and Scoffing" above), with which he won important people over to his viewpoint.

Evidently the widow did not want to keep mitzvot — which is why Moshe repeatedly told her, "Be careful." With this story, Korah was arguing: Mitzvot are meant to connect us to Hashem. This is not accomplished when force or rebuke is used. You can try convincing the widow, but if she still refuses, leave her alone; it's her own problem.

Korah convinced important people that his viewpoint was correct, for it is surely better to do mitzvot out of love for Hashem than out of fear of a human leader.

Korah's opinion will be instituted — but only in the Messianic era. At that time, there will be no evil inclination, so serving Hashem will not be a challenge.[38] No one will be forced to keep mitzvot, "for the earth will be filled with knowledge of Hashem."[39]

Thus in *Mizmor Shir leyom HaShabbat*,[40] we find the words *tzaddik catamar yifrah*, "A tzaddik will flourish like a date palm."[41] Says the Rokeah:[42] The last letters of the Hebrew words spell Korah (קרח), to hint that in the Messianic era, Hashem will take Korah out of Gehinnom and seat him in a place of honor.

But until Mashiah comes, we have an evil inclination, and the

37. See *Sanhedrin* 109b.
38. See Kohelet 12:1, *Kohelet Rabbah*..
39. Yeshayahu 11:9.
40. Tehilim 92.
41. Tehilim 92:13.
42. Commentary on the Siddur, 24.

gedol hador must stand guard and prevent breaches. If this widow stops giving the charity and gifts required by the Torah, so will her neighbors, and then her neighbors' neighbors, until society disintegrates. Long before we had kings, Hashem entrusted the authority to stop any violations to our Torah leaders, whom we must obey unquestioningly.

THE ORDER OF EVENTS

Those who died in the plague were 14,700, aside from those who died because of the episode of Korah.[43]

The sorry episode of Korah did not happen in a vacuum. It was preceded by the episode of the Spies, who in turn failed to learn a lesson from what happened to Miriam — all this in three consecutive Parshiot.

Parashat Behaalotecha ends with the punishment of Miriam. The righteous prophetess was the first to think she could give Moshe Rabbenu advice. She criticized him for separating from his wife, and said: Hashem agreed only after he did it of his own volition. And she felt that Mosheshould not have done so. We are also prophets, and yet Hashem did not command us to separate from our spouses![44]

Miriam, who loved her brother, Moshe, spoke only to their holy brother, Aaron, and only out of concern for Moshe's well-being. Nevertheless, she was stricken with *tzaraat*.

Parashat Shelah begins with the Spies, who should have learned from what happened to Miriam, but they didn't. They thought they could give Moshe advice (see "The 'Advice' of the Spies" in Shelah).

---

43. Bamidbar 17:14.
44. See also Tosaphot and Rabbenu Tam.

The Spies died a miserable death, caused the Jews to wander in the desert for forty years, and sowed the seeds for the destruction of the First and Second Temples.

Parashat Korah tells about a man who thought he knew better than Moshe.

Korah and his group were burned and swallowed up by the earth, following which a plague claimed the lives of another 14,700 Jews.

Says the Gemara:[45] Whoever thinks ill of his Rav, it is as if he thinks ill of the *Shechinah*.

We must revere and humbly obey our Torah leaders, and certainly never criticize them or think we know better.

---

45. *Sanhedrin* 110a.